Relationship Tools
for Positive Change

HOW TO TRANSFORM
ISSUES OR UPSETS INTO
OPPORTUNITIES TO
STRENGTHEN

BY JOHN GREY, PH.D.

LEAP FROG PRESS

To Bonney

CODEVELOPER OF MATERIAL IN THIS BOOK
PARTNER IN RELATIONSHIP RESEARCH
FRIEND AND FELLOW TRAVELER
ON A PATH OF GROWTH

RELATIONSHIP TOOLS FOR POSITIVE CHANGE

Copyright © 2005 by John Grey, Ph.D.

For information write:

LEAP FROG PRESS
501 Swain Avenue
Sebastopol, CA 95472

website : www.soulmateoracle.com

John Grey, Ph.D. provides relationship coaching by phone to people throughout the U.S. He also offers a unique weekend retreat for couples to clarify and transform their relationships. Information about all of the author's coaching services—as well as many free self-help tools and a way to contact the author—can be found at the following website:

http://www. soulmateoracle.com

CONTENTS

What takes us from the high of love to the low of falling
into a hole filled with upsetting problems? See how we
can only resolve relationship issues outside of this hole.

How we view our issues can keep us from solving them.
By setting a conscious intention, we can turn problems
into vital opportunities to build love and trust.

Personal baggage limits our ability to resolve issues and
causes suffering in love. It's vital to take stock of how
we react and the emotional coping strategies we use.

Our personality type affects our ability to succeed in a
longterm relationship. We need to clearly see the box
we are in, to get beyond its negative limitations.

Differences may first attract, but then lead us to polarize
and have upsetting issues. Declare an end to the war and
start working with personal differences.

The basic rule when things are not working is to do
something different! Here are fundamental shifts you
can make to change an unhappy relationship pattern.

What's rule one if you fall into a hole? Stop digging!
Here's a vital communication tool to keep yourself from
damaging a relationship over problems or upsets.

Learn a key tool to center yourself, stay alert, maximize
your resourcefulness, and act your best in any situation.

Good communication is a vital ingredient to keep love
and happiness strong. Learn a critical tool to get positive
results when you communicate.

We can get stuck in upset feelings. Learn a useful way
to move through negative emotional states, release upset
feelings and heal old wounds.

Join in sharing the mutual goals of personal growth and
relationship growth. Agree to take a new path if upsets
or challenges arise, one that strengthens your love.

Relationship Coaching by Phone
Couples Retreats

PREFACE

Many couples start out with the magical feelings of falling in love. At the start of a new relationship, people often feel they have found the "one"—that special person who could be a loving partner for life.

Given such a strong start, one wonders how anything could ever go wrong. But as we all know, the magic doesn't last forever. The road to "happily ever after" has more than a few rocks, potholes and bumps along the way.

This is the part they don't show at the movies. Hollywood is a good presenter of they myths we share as a society about relationships. Have you ever noticed how the end credits roll once the leading couple finally comes together?

Movies reflect our fairy tales about perfect love. The focus is on getting to the bliss of the honeymoon. When we view relationships this way, we think that the "right" person—by definition—is someone who never upsets us, someone who always makes us feel good. It's just like magic!

In fact, for most people, the sense of magic ends the day that problems, differences or upsetting issues appear. Many *potential* life partners get lost in problems. They wonder if they are with the right person, because they are feeling upset instead of joyful.

The popular myths of love do not educate us about what to do with problems, upsets or differences. We have all heard that "relationships take work." But what exactly *is* that work? Most of us have never witnessed how a couple can deal with upset in a way that strengthens their love.

As we enter into adult relationships, we have not learned from any great models that demonstrated healthy relating in the face of problems.

We enter our relationships without a full set of tools and understandings essential to longterm success. We are not well equipped to handle the problems, issues, differences and challenges that await us in adult relationships.

Though we may deny it intellectually, on an emotional level we still unconsciously hold onto to the myth of perfect love—where upsetting things "shouldn't happen" and are a sign we are not "right" for each other.

We still have in front of us the task of learning what it takes to keep love strong in the face of challenges—to traverse the holes and obstacles on a couple's path so we don't just end up another relationship "on the rocks."

So when the magic of the honeymoon period comes to an end, it is vital to learn to do things differently—to learn what it takes to maintain lasting, resilient, healthy love.

We have to throw out a lot of old ways of thinking. We have to examine our myths.

We have to forge a new path.

That path will change our lives for the better.

This book was created to teach you practical relationship tools. Its aim is to equip you with the essential knowledge and skills to deal with real-world relationship issues, navigate problems or upsets, communicate well, get positive results and create the kind of loving partnership you truly want.

To Your Success and Happiness in Love,
John Grey, Ph.D.

CHAPTER ONE
BEYOND THE HONEYMOON

"The course of true love never did run smooth."
—SHAKESPEARE

The deep yearning to share life with someone moves most of us toward relationship. Our hearts dream of a union that will add sparkle to the experience of being.

When we fall in love, we find bliss and inspiration. It can be like sailing to a tropical island paradise. We are exploring new territory—the magnificently unfamiliar. We are in the honeymoon of a new beginning

The honeymoon is a time of magic and wonder. We feel alive with excitement, curiosity and new possibility. We want to share each possible moment with our newly found love.

- **Open**
- **Exciting**
- **Sharing**
- **Adventurous**
- **Curious**
- **Receptive**

Hearts open. Spirits soar. The sun is shining brightly. We are filled with hope. We are undeniably altered, transcendent and expansive.

Unfortunately, the honeymoon does not last indefinitely. There is another phase of relating that soon follows. This is a part Hollywood seldom shows. It's the theme of mournful love songs. It starts when the honeymoon ends.

We all know that sooner or later the honeymoon is over. It may last weeks, months, or even years. But it does end at some point. And then another phase of relationship begins....

WHAT HAPPENS WHEN
"The honeymoon is over!"

What happens? A return to reality? Is "real life" finally entering the equation? Does love somehow just slip away?

Sadly, many couples look back at their honeymoon period only to feel a loss. The rest of their time together never quite measures up to it. Sometimes people will leave relationships in favor of finding another honeymoon high.

If we go around that merry-go-round one too many times, we may get cynical from repeated honeymoons turned into heartbreaks. We conclude that falling in love is an illusion to be avoided—and guard our heart.

In fact, the honeymoon shows us something real. But it is difficult to accept the gift for what it truly is.

The honeymoon gives us a glimpse of possibility for ourselves in love. It shows us the potential for a relationship. How can we make good on that possibility—and turn the potential into a lasting reality?

We must first understand what ends the honeymoon. If we look closely, we will see how a relationship unconsciously slips across a threshold from happiness into suffering. We will see the mechanisms involved. This will give vital information for what to do differently—to keep love strong and growing.

When we fall in love, we experience a state which takes us beyond normal reality. We expand, unexpectedly, into a fullness and spaciousness of being.

We may feel like flowers opening to the sunshine of love. But in fact, that sun resides in us, and we are lighting it up. We shine it onto everything we see and that changes our world.

We are truly operating "outside the box."

This is a gift and a mystery.

But then, something upsetting happens and we contract. The light seems to go out. We start feeling differently. We collapse back to our normal mode, back into the box.

Is it possible to choose to get outside the box again? It will have to be an act of conscious choice. That is a choice worth making, and learning more about.

To empower ourselves to make this choice, we start by examining the box—and what pulls us into it. We look at the "bad" stuff that happens in love, and where it comes from.

Normally we avoid thinking about this. Such avoidance is what keeps us in the box. But in seeing the box more clearly, we can also see how to get out of it.

Thus we start by looking at what happens when the honeymoon is over. Ultimately, seeing this clearly will open our eyes to new choices, keys to lasting love.

SIGNS THE HONEYMOON IS OVER

• Problems
• Challenges ⎫ Conventional Wisdom:
• Upsets ⎬ These are normally seen as
• Differences ⎭ "negative" signs

Couples usually declare the honeymoon is over when *problems, challenges, upsets* or *differences* arise.

These are normally seen as negative signs—signs that something is "wrong"—signs of a "bad" relationship.

Most couples will look for the "cause" of these unwanted events. Inevitably, they point the finger at each other. Getting the other person to change is seen as the way back to the wonderful expanded feelings of the honeymoon.

Predictably, this fails. And instead of getting back to the expanded state, both people find themselves contracting.

This is not a conscious strategy. It is a knee-jerk reaction. Seeing a problem, challenge, upset or differences as a negative sign is the typical thing to do, the conventional wisdom.

It is rare to find people who greet problems by saying "Wow, this is great! We can really grow here!" But to succeed longterm, we do need to embrace relationship challenges with a different mindset. This means learning to view our issues differently than unwanted negative signs.

Unconsciously, most of us *do* see things according to the conventional wisdom. We may feel that "differences attract" at first meeting. But after the honeymoon, people normally start to complain about how "unlike me" the other person is. There's a tendency to see the other person as "wrong" or deficient in character, because they are different.

Let's look at the underlying process that turns problems and differences into road blocks to lasting love.

VICIOUS CIRCLE

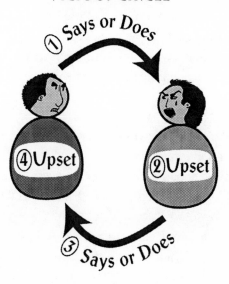

We call it the Vicious Circle. It is the basic pattern that runs a relationship into the ground. Here's how it works:

(1) A person says or does something—and...

(2) The other person gets upset—then...

(3) That person says or does something in return—and...

(4) The first person gets upset.

Around and around the circle we go, spinning faster and faster. In a matter of minutes we can heat up—or go stone cold. It can take days or weeks to recover.

Here's an example. This was the defining moment when Sarah and Michael knew their honeymoon was over. They were driving to a meeting with a friend that was going to be hard for her. She was unusually quiet and inward.

Noticing this, Michael wanted to lighten things up and relieve the tension. He tried to inject a little humor the way he normally did with his friends, by lightly teasing her. Sarah remained quiet, so he continued to try to draw her out by teasing. Suddenly, she blew up and called him insensitive.

Michael reacted with sarcasm, which was not received any better than the teasing had been. He said she was ruining the trip and blamed her for not responding to his good intentions like his friends would have.

This gave evidence to the old saying that the road to hell is paved with good intentions.

Only minutes had passed and they were going around the Vicious Circle with increasing speed. This was their first fight. They stayed upset over it for a week.

The Vicious Circle can also be seen as a Downward Spiral, that takes you to what we call the "Hole." As this happens, there are a number of things that couples, not acting at their best, typically say or do.

You will often hear one person blaming the other for causing the situation. Like, "You make me angry!"

You may hear name calling. One person calls the other "insensitive" or "selfish" or some other negative label.

There are classic red-flag words—"always," "never,"

DOWNWARD SPIRAL

SAY
Blame
the Other
Person

"Always"
"Never"
"Should"
"Right"
"Wrong"

"You Make
Me Angry!"

DO
Explode
Distance
Pursue
Retreat

SAY
Label
the Other
Person

"You are
Selfish!"

"You are
so Lazy!"

"You are
Insensitive"

THE HOLE

"should," "right" and "wrong"—words that reveal that the mind is narrowing or getting lost in judgments.

Behind such words, the emotional arena has collapsed into a basic reaction of "fight or flight." There may be anger or pursuit, distancing or retreat. Depending upon the couple, things can get explosive—or stone cold.

Couples in the Hole are dominated by their reactivity. The

"fight or flight" reaction powerfully alters body-brain chemistry. It's the chemistry that ancient humans needed to battle or escape a tiger suddenly appearing in the jungle. In relationship, this chemical reaction fundamentally changes how we talk and act. It is like being very intoxicated. Very very intoxicated. The chemicals have taken over.

This is important to realize. When you are in the Hole— you are *under the influence*. As the brain's chemical balance shifts in preparation for "fight or flight," our pulse rate and breathing alters, our perception narrows, and our mental capacity collapses into black and white thinking.

Statements get dramatized and overgeneralized. You hear things like, "You *never* help me around here!" "I'm *always* cleaning up after you!"

In the Hole, our positive options are sharply reduced—if not gone altogether. Yet, people keep trying to resolve the situation, as if they could! Each wants to put in the final word. Emotions escalate. Someone may explode or leave.

Most couples can recognize their own version of being in the Hole. One question I have repeatedly asked is:

"Has there ever been one time when you were in the Hole and able to work things out in a successful way?"

I have yet to hear a single story of any such success.

Nor am I likely to, for a very good reason: solving an interpersonal issue takes skill.

Would you do brain surgery if you were totally drunk? Then why try to negotiate an important issue when you are under the influence of the chemistry of "fight or flight"?

What results when you try to solve things after you fall into the Hole? No matter how hard you might try to "work" on things, if you're in the Hole, you can only make matters worse. This is "work" that absolutely *does not work.* The things you do in the Hole are what *destroy* a relationship.

IN THE HOLE YOU ONLY DESTROY LOVE

- Blame the other person
- Label the other person
- Criticize the other person
- See them as the cause of your feelings
- Be defensive
- Stonewall, shut down & distance
- Win-Lose, "right" vs. "wrong"

BLAME: "You ruined our entire vacation!"
LABEL: "You are weak!" "You're such a slob!"
CRITICIZE: "You're self-centered!" "You are needy!"
CAUSE: "You frustrate me!" "You make me upset!"
DEFENSIVE: "That's your problem!"
                  "What about when you..."
STONEWALL: Walk out. Avoid the issue.
WIN-LOSE: "You're wrong!" "You never do it right."

Most of us can recognize one or more of these. They seem like normal things to do when upset. But be warned. This is exactly what takes a relationship from happiness into suffering. We react these ways unconsciously—and we destroy love.

Unless we develop different strategies to resolve issues, the strategies of the Hole will either destroy a partnership, or leave us sharing long term unhappiness.

In my coaching practice, when I first meet couples I often hear statements from the Hole. Each person makes a case for how they are right, how the other person needs to change.

I ask, "Would you rather be right—or happy?"

If you want happiness, read the last sentence again. Then commit that question to memory!

Emotionally intelligent people only attempt to resolve issues when they are outside the Hole. If they find they are moving toward the Hole, they will stop, and find a way to get centered. They will continue discussing the issue later when they can be more constructive.

If you want lasting love, you need to avoid the Hole and its destructive influence. Remember rule one if you find yourself in a deep, dark Hole—*Stop Digging!*

Next we will look at what *is* effective if you want to solve interpersonal issues. These are keys for building longterm happiness and keeping love strong.

OUTSIDE THE HOLE YOU RESOLVE ISSUES

- Be curious about the other person
- See your own part in things
- Own and self-care for your feelings
- Listen to the other's viewpoint
- Open to hear what's true for them
- Consider their sensitivities
- Win-Win, mutual solutions

BE CURIOUS ABOUT THE OTHER PERSON. Instead of trying to LABEL or CRITICIZE your partner, you become *curious* about what is happening inside of them. Suspending your own judgments, you ask them what is going on for them. You then will learn something new about them, and they won't feel under attack.

SEE YOUR OWN PART IN THINGS. Instead of putting the BLAME on them for the situation, you *see your own part* in how things developed. This gives you an active role in changing things, and empowers you to avoid similar traps in the future.

OWN AND SELF-CARE FOR YOUR FEELINGS. Instead of making them the CAUSE of what you feel, you *own* your feelings. Instead of needing them to change in order to fix how you feel, you begin to learn to *self-care* for and heal your emotional states.

LISTEN TO THE OTHER'S VIEWPOINT. Instead of getting DEFENSIVE over what your partner may be saying, you just *listen*. You get to understand their viewpoint and learn more about their sensitivities. This helps you avoid hot buttons in the future.

OPEN TO HEAR WHAT'S TRUE FOR THEM. Instead of starting to STONEWALL or CLOSE DOWN, you *open* to hear what is true for your partner. They feel heard, understood and accepted as human beings. This is a basic requirement for a relationship to grow and prosper.

CONSIDER THEIR SENSITIVITIES. Instead of being exclusively focused on your own needs and feelings, you can also consider the other person's sensitivities, as well. Partners who work things out together well have developed a map of each other's hot buttons and sensitivities. They know how to avoid setting off emotional landmines.

WIN-WIN MUTUAL SOLUTION. Instead of a WIN-LOSE outcome, you are interested in finding a *mutually* satisfactory solution. You will take into account the other person's needs. This enables you to co-create happiness together on an ongoing and lasting basis.

Unfortunately, a majority of us have not been exposed to many positive strategies for dealing with issues from outside the Hole. We probably did not see many of these constructive ways of relating when we were growing up.

This is one reason that today there are a lot of unhappy couples who mainly deal with issues from inside of the Hole. Until we consciously learn to do something different, we just repeat the relationship strategies we saw or developed in our childhood. How many of us had the good fortune to be shown constructive relating skills early in life? Consider the lucky child in the following story:

There was once a small boy who found a green turtle. He started to examine it but then the turtle pulled in its head and closed its shell tight like a vice. The boy was upset, so he picked up a stick to try to pry it open.

The boy's father saw this and remarked, "No, son, that's not the way! In fact, you may poke at it—and even kill the turtle—but you'll never get it to open up with a stick."

His father took the turtle indoors and set it near the fireplace. It wasn't but a few minutes until it began to get warm. Then the turtle pushed out its head, stretched out its legs and began to crawl.

"Turtles are like that," said the father, "and people, too. You can't force them into anything by poking at them. But if you first warm them up with some real kindness, more than likely, they will open and come out of their shell."

What a lucky child to be taught an important lesson: use skillful relating instead of poking or using force. Otherwise people close up and get defensive.

So what if we didn't get taught such positive lessons in childhood—by word or example? This only means that we have to learn them now.

The good news is that these new skills *can* be learned.

Curiosity is a powerful skill

Perhaps the most powerful skill we can ever develop is to be *curious* in a challenging situation. This is an inner strength. It is staying open to possibility—not investing in what you think you already know.

"Knowing" is the cement that permanently seals in our misery. It kills love. We know exactly how our partner feels, and what they mean by their words or actions. We couldn't possibly be misinterpreting them. In fact, we don't even realize that's all we are doing—*interpreting* them.

Nothing closes us down faster than being misinterpreted or told what we feel. It's a ticket straight to the Hole.

THE FIVE STAGES OF GROWTH

Here's a little story that illustrates how we learn new and better strategies. We learn through trail and error, in stages:

STAGE 1. You're walking down a road and there's a hole. You fall into the hole. You think, "Who put this hole here? Why did they do this to me? I don't deserve this treatment..." You scratch and dig... and finally, with cuts and bruises... you get out of the hole and continue walking...

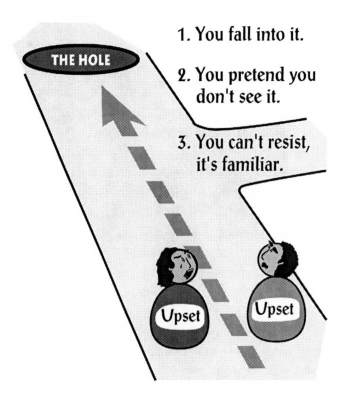

THE HOLE

1. You fall into it.

2. You pretend you don't see it.

3. You can't resist, it's familiar.

Upset   Upset

STAGE 2. You're walking down a road and there's a hole. You pretend that you don't see it. You act as if it isn't really there. So you fall into the hole. You think, "Who put this here? How can they keep doing this to me? This isn't right! They are wrong..." You scratch and dig... and with cuts and bruises... you get out of the hole and continue walking...

STAGE 3. You're walking down a road and there's a hole. You see it. But you just can't resist. It's so familiar... that you jump into the hole. You now think, "How come I always end up here? What is this hole really all about?" You scratch and dig... and finally, with cuts and bruises... you get out of the hole and continue walking...

STAGE 4. You're walking down a road and there's a hole. You see it. You recognize it. You've been in that hole before. You think, "I know this hole! I don't want to go in there..." So you walk around the hole and continue walking...

THE HOLE

4. You walk around the hole.

STAGE 5. You're walking down a road and there's a hole. You know that road. You've gone down that road before. You think, "This is the road with the hole in it." So you go down a new road and continue walking...

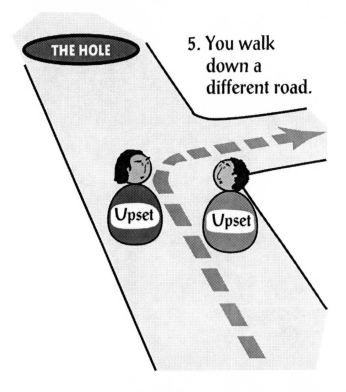

THE HOLE

5. You walk down a different road.

Upset

Upset

The parable illustrates the five stages of positive growth in how we deal with issues, problems or upsets. At first we just find ourselves in a deep hole, and blame someone else for putting us there. Next, we see it but deny it, and fall in again. Third, we see it more clearly, but it seems so familiar and compelling that we jump back in once more.

We start making progress when we see the hole and just walk around it. Finally, we decide to go down a different road altogether. We move toward the unfamiliar, new and unknown. This is the journey of personal and relationship growth.

Most of us can easily identify with the story of the Hole. When couples start working with me, I ask which "Stage" they currently are in. It's usually Stage 3.

I then show couples how to move beyond the grip of the Hole and learn to explore new territory.

The tools offered later in this book will keep you out of the Hole. They are the methods wise partners use to deal with potentially upsetting situations.

We next examine what makes the Hole so familiar and compelling that, even when a couple sees it clearly, they still find themselves jumping in.

WHAT PULLS US INTO THE HOLE?

We unconsciously follow a "map" into the Hole. This map was formed in our past, drawn from personal history.

Think of the map as a metaphor for how the brain learns, organizes and stores our experiences. Our developmental learning process is like the creation of internal maps. Adults use many maps developed in childhood. We have a map for the English language and a map of the letters of the alphabet as visual building blocks of words. These maps enable you to read what you are now reading.

Similarly, we have a map for how to interpret behaviors of others—and how to react. These maps are not always accurate. We easily misinterpret the actions or intentions of others, and our reactions do not represent who we are at our best.

Parts of our map take us to the Hole. Especially parts that reference emotional triggers and hot buttons, sensitivities and past wounds, family conditioning, negative beliefs and limiting communication styles.

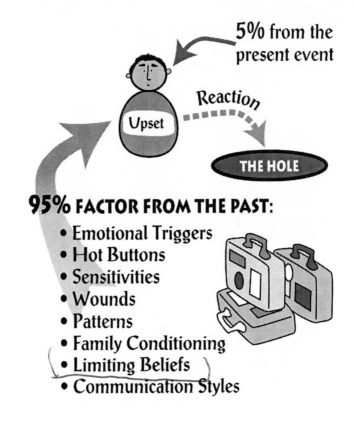

5% from the present event

Reaction

Upset

THE HOLE

95% FACTOR FROM THE PAST:
- **Emotional Triggers**
- **Hot Buttons**
- **Sensitivities**
- **Wounds**
- **Patterns**
- **Family Conditioning**
- **Limiting Beliefs**
- **Communication Styles**

I call these elements the "95% factor" from the past. Another name for it is "baggage." We bring our baggage into new relationships. When something today activates part of our old baggage, we can be taken to the Hole. At such times, we can feel out of control. We suddenly are in the Hole, doing and saying things we would not have done if we were in a calmer, more resourceful state.

There is added emotional intensity in the Hole. This is what the 95% factor refers to. It is like an emotional amplifier. It turns up the volume of our reaction, boosting us into a state where we can no longer be constructive.

Another way of looking at the 95% factor is to ask, "Is this emotional response proportional to the event at hand?"

When we are in the Hole, usually only 5% of our emotional energy is proportional to the present event. The rest is about the past. The reactions we are having may not even have anything to do with our present partner.

Recall the example of Sarah and Michael driving to a meeting, where she was being unusually quiet. When he tried to lighten things up by teasing her, she blew up and called him insensitive.

If Sarah's response had been proportional to the event in the car, it may have had only 5% of that emotional energy. At a 5% level, she might have simply said, "Michael, this meeting is on my mind. I need some time to be quiet and prepare for it." Or she might have said, "Please don't tease me. I really don't like being teased."

Instead, the 95% factor from Sarah's past kicked in. Experiencing a big jolt of emotion, she became enraged. Perceiving Michael as the sole cause of her feeling, she made a negative judgment. This, in turn, seemed to him like an unprovoked attack and he became defensive.

They went straight to the Hole.

So what was in Sarah's map from the past? It turned out that the 95% factor was that in childhood, her father often ridiculed Sarah with putdowns in the form of teasing.

Michael unwittingly hit that land mine.

THE MAP FROM OUR PAST HISTORY

The map from the past that takes us to the Hole was created by events where we ended up feeling bad or thinking less of ourselves. These events could have been about something big or little.

The feelings from these events were never healed or resolved, and they continue to influence us today. They are reactivated by anything today that reminds us of the original events in the past.

This is the 95% factor. It is primed and ready to amplify any of the emotional responses we have today.

Unfortunately, most of us are unskilled at noticing when the 95% factor kicks in. We don't question the accuracy of our interpretation of the present event. We don't ask how the past is influencing our perception. We may even tend to mistake the strength of our reaction with its accuracy—so the stronger we feel, the more right we are!

If only 5% of Sarah's emotional energy was truly needed for the event in the car, then why couldn't she have just stopped at that and delivered a constructive message to get what she really wanted?

Most likely, she had no idea that she had ever moved beyond the level of appropriate response. Few of us recognize that we are going beyond 5% when it is happening. Perhaps we continue to feel we are responding proportionally, all the way to the Hole.

We all have maps from the past. It's important to admit that you can be reactive. Become alert to see when you are operating beyond the 5% level. Know that even at 10% you are in danger, because it's a short jump to the Hole.

THE GOOD NEWS

The map is not the territory

The good news is that the *map* is not the *territory.*

How we think things are is not the same as how they really are or what is possible for us to experience.

We do not have to stay limited by our maps. We can learn new things throughout life. To achieve a deep, lasting happiness, you are called on to expand your current map. If you want to go somewhere other than the Hole, you need to discover a new road.

The good news is that you *can* travel on new roads in a

relationship. It can be done! All kinds of new roads are there for you to discover. And the tools in this book will help you find and share them with a loving partner.

Wise partners are open to taking new roads where the old one only leads to the Hole. Consider the following metaphor about the difference between Heaven and Hell.

In Hell, you are taken into a room where there is a giant table full of all manner of wonderful food for a feast. Around the table sit the residents of Hell, frantically scooping up the food. They are using big spoons which are permanently fastened to their hands. But the handles on each spoon are a bit longer than their arms. So they can never reach the ends of the spoon back to their mouths. They are literally starving at a feast, slopping food all over themselves—screaming and moaning with the pain of starvation!

In Heaven, you are taken into a similar room with a giant table set with the food for a feast. Around that table sit the occupants of Heaven. They too have spoons fastened to their hands, each with handles longer than their arms. But here, with their long spoons, these people are feeding each other! Sounds of pleasure and happiness abound.

This is a feast fit for life partners, who know how to travel on a new road and discover mutually satisfying solutions— even in the most challenging of situations.

So the good news is that the map is *not* the territory. We *can* expand and we *can* learn new skills and attitudes that will improve the quality of our love life. Even if we acquired poor strategies in childhood, we can learn new things now.

It takes conscious intention to do this learning. It is vital to know from the start what we are up against.

THE BAD NEWS

- **The map is unconscious**
- **We follow it automatically**
- **It's what is familiar to us**
- **We mistake our map for reality**

We acquired our map in childhood. Between two and eight years old, we learned most of the ways we negatively react to other people. We learned how to interpret others, when to get upset, and how to express it, or hide it. We came to conclusions as to how the world is, and how we must deal with it.

The conclusions we made and conditioning we received in childhood reside mainly in our unconscious minds. As adults, we are affected by these on a daily basis, in ways we do not directly recognize.

The power of the unconscious is enormous, everpresent. Think of a fish in a bowl of water. Viewed from outside, we can see the fish, the water, the bowl. But if you are the fish, can you see the water? No. Your whole world simply is water, and so you cannot differentiate water from anything else.

This is partly why it is so easy for us to see our partner's hangups, old baggage and needless emotional reactions—but we don't tend to observe our own.

Many of the things we learned in childhood still serve us well. We learned to walk and talk. We learned to look both ways before crossing the street, and to wait for the light to turn green. We now do these things automatically.

But a lot of things learned in childhood are not still so beneficial. These are the things which take us to the Hole—the ways we negatively interpret the words and actions of others, the ways in which we believe we must react to them.

We easily mistake our map for reality. When we are upset, we mistake our interpretations for what is really going on. We place our partner somewhere in our unconscious past, and mistake that for who they really are. We label them and believe we know just what their intentions and feelings are.

In other words, we turn our partners into co-stars in our old movies. In the example above, Sarah cast Michael to play the role of the abusive father in her old movie. An old script written long ago determined how she reacted to his teasing in the car. Most likely, she didn't consciously realize this. She just reacted, as if he were being abusive.

Sarah made a snap judgment, as we are prone to do.

It can be called the map, our old movies, or our baggage. It can be called our personality patterns of emotional reactivity. We are limited by it. It affects how we react to each other and how we end up in the Hole.

Do you really think you are actively choosing to get upset? Are you operating at your best when upset? Are you being the person you truly want to be? Are you choosing, as an adult, to blow up at or shrink away from your partner?

Or would it be more accurate to say you are overcome by the urge, the feeling, the need to do so? Where does that come from, if you are not actively choosing it?

In a real sense, we are put into a box by this map from the past—our personality patterns, our emotional coping strategies. Adult relationships eventually put in front of our eyes most of the unconscious self-limiting patterns we have been carrying since childhood. We can see these in the ways in which we get upset and suffer in love.

At a certain time in adult life, we may choose to wake up, stay alert, and not mistake our maps for reality. We may yearn to get out of the box, to delete our old tapes, to travel a new road—pick your favorite metaphor.

One can start this awakening by becoming wary of making snap judgments. Delay judging an event or situation. Find within you the ability to be curious—and the courage to not think you already know what is going on.

In order to get out of the box, it is vital to first see the box we are already in. Freedom starts with knowledge of the truth. The old saying, "Know Thyself", is a path to freedom.

IN OUR HEARTS, WE WANT FREEDOM!

- **Expand beyond limits of map**
- **Heal old wounds**
- **Realize our dreams of love**

In our hearts, we ache for freedom. We want to heal old wounds and expand beyond the limits based on the past. We want to realize our dreams and potential for love today.

We get a brief taste of this expansion during the initial period of a relationship—during the magic and wonder of the honeymoon. Love opens us.

The honeymoon is like a vacation. Our usual limits are transcended. The magical sense of this time is an experience of living beyond our normal maps. It's a visit to a wonderful foreign place.

In the honeymoon, we get a glimpse of our expanded

selves. This gives us a snapshot of possibility. It is not just an illusion or a projection. During this time, we are operating as our expanded selves—outside the box.

The fairy tales we secretly harbor about "true love" are derived from this phase of relating. When we fall in love, most of us take it as direct evidence that we are finally involved in the "real thing" with the "right person." We may feel so strongly that we believe we have met our "soulmate."

But eventually we find out we don't travel that light... We carry old "Baggage"

When we rediscover our old baggage, the honeymoon is over. We collapse back into our typical patterns of reaction and emotional contraction.

The arrival of baggage seems like a rude catastrophe, a sign that love has taken a turn for the worse. We may even conclude we are with the "wrong person."

Few couples understand that relationship moves in stages. Old baggage is certain to be rediscovered until it gets healed. In fact, old baggage and wounds may even be emerging into the light of new love in order to be healed.

Here's a little-known secret:

Love brings up anything unlike itself... to be healed and transformed

What's unlike love? Pain—old wounds—deep fears—negative beliefs—all the ingredients of the 95% factor from the past. Love often brings up old baggage for healing. Love brings up our old patterns of emotional reactivity—because these reside in us and want to be transformed.

Expansion and growth can be an integral part of a loving relationship. Can you see this potential? As a start, do not deny old baggage. Begin to realize its arrival signals an important moment—where old wounds can be healed, old limits can be surpassed, and old emotional patterns can be transformed.

This realization can come suddenly, as it did for Susan. She had been a client for six months, and every week she arrived with a new story of how her boyfriend Paul upset her. She complained about his lack of sensitivity, his inability to express feelings, his unconsciousness in spending time together, and his lack of visual awareness—he was a "slob." She was doing the blame game, saying everything would be great if Paul would just get his act together.

We approached these multiple challenges in a variety of ways, to come to a deeper understanding of what it was that was really upsetting her. She continued to insist that it was all Paul and that she had nothing to do with it. After six months of exploring the same challenges over and over, without the results she was looking for, I gently leaned forward in my chair, and said "Perhaps Paul is not the man for you."

She leapt out of her chair and responded, "How can you say that? He is perfect for me! Nobody pushes my buttons like he does. And if he doesn't push my buttons, how will I ever grow?" She relaxed back into her chair, having an expression conveying that a light just went on in her head.

I said, "Great! Now we can start talking about something that will really make a difference."

From that point on, we began to use issues as ways to self-understanding and healing. She changed her focus to her own personal growth, rather than placing the blame on Paul.

She expanded her ability to be aware of what she was feeling, what she needed and wanted, and how to communicate these in a respectful way.

We also explored where her reactive triggers and hot buttons came from and how to move beyond them.

In essence, she began to get out of the box that had limited her in relationships, once she turned her focus around from Paul to where she could grow.

We have all heard that "relationships take work."

Unfortunately, nobody ever explained to us exactly what that work was. There is a simple saying we like—one which sounds odd, but rings true. It clarifies what some of the most important, overlooked work is:

Relationship is an inside job

Our main work is to turn our attention to where it normally is not—on our own role in the relationship, and what we can do to create positive change. This is the only way to discover our own true power within a relationship.

We are only pretending we have no affect if we think it is our partner is at fault for how things are. As long as we focus on the other person, we give up our power and keep ourselves stuck inside our own limited box.

The most important shift we can make is paradoxical. It is to put our attention on ourselves, and how we need to get out of our own box. This is the path to freeing ourselves—and our relationships—to grow.

CHAPTER TWO

SEE WHERE YOU WANT TO GO

*"If you don't know where you are going,
any road will get you there."*—LEWIS CARROLL

How you view events affects how you respond.

Say you are waiting in a line at a movie. Suddenly, some guy in a heavy coat crashes his way through the line, steps on your foot, never looks back, but just keeps marching along. How do you think you'd react to this?

Next, the person in front of you points out that the guy has a white cane and is bumping into other people. His head turns to the side, and you indeed see he has dark glasses on. What would your reaction be to this new information?

Finally, the person in line behind you says, "That guy comes crashing through here every night. He carries that cane, just pretending to be blind, so he can get away with it." Okay, now what do you think your reaction would be?

With each new view of what is happening, your response may significantly change. The same thing is true in love and relationship. How you view what is going on determines the way in which you will respond.

When a challenge or upset occurs, how you view it may point you down the road toward the Hole. But a different view of what is happening may point you to a new road that may lead to resolving the issue and increasing happiness.

How you see a relationship problem directly affects how you act—and how you succeed or fail to resolve it.

How you view an issue, challenge or upset comes down to one all-important question. Here's the bottom line:

Do you see it as a problem—or an opportunity?

Is it a Problem... or an Opportunity?

How you view Challenges & Upset determines the road you'll take.

Is the glass half empty or half full? If your focus is on the emptiness, you may needlessly die of thirst. If you focus on its fullness, you can drink, nurture and refresh yourself.

The Chinese language contains many written symbols that have complementary meanings. The most well-known of such Chinese characters is "Wei ji"—the symbol for crisis.

This character for "crisis" actually consists of two parts: one represents "danger"—the other means "opportunity."

Whether you see a challenge in terms of being an unwanted problem or a meaningful opportunity will dramatically impact your response. If you see it in negative terms, the energy you bring into the relationship will also be negative.

Since challenges and upsets are inevitable, your viewpoint will make a big difference as to whether your relationship will grow in a positive direction, or get stuck in the Hole.

"Nothing is good or bad, but thinking makes it so," the old master said. When asked to explain he said, "A devout man cheerfully observed a religious fast for seven days. However, his neighbor starved to death on the same diet."

THE CONVENTIONAL WISDOM

Most of us look at challenges, upsets or differences as a "bad" sign. These are seen as unwanted interruptions to love and happiness.

This conventional viewpoint is how a majority of people see relationship challenges. It's what we hear from our family and friends, from songs and movies.

This is a viewpoint we never consciously choose. We are not even aware that we could have a choice! It is like water to a fish, or air to a bird. It is just the way things are—how could they be any different?

The normal viewpoint is that problems mean something is *wrong*. Often we conclude that it's something "wrong" with our partner, who is seen as the cause of the upset.

We may even conclude that something is "wrong" with the

relationship. Or, if we tend to take blame ourselves, we may conclude there's something "wrong" with us.

It means that "SOMETHING IS WRONG" with the Relationship... or You... or Me...

This is undesirable... need to fix it... get rid of it... or get distance...

Wherever it is located—in your partner, the relationship or yourself—something is definitely "wrong." Whatever it is, it is undesirable. Your intention becomes to fix it, change it, get rid of it, or get distance from it—and the relationship.

If we conclude the "something wrong" is located in our partner, then we usually end up blaming or criticizing. If we think it might be located in ourselves, we may get defensive. If we believe "something is wrong" with the relationship, we may close off and distance ourselves.

Reacting to the vision that "something is wrong" does the actual damage to love. Blaming, criticizing, defending and shutting down are the destroyers of a relationship.

As soon as challenges or upsets are seen as a "bad" sign everything else follows. You will think something is "wrong" and need to figure out who to "blame."

Seeing an upset or challenge as a "bad" sign only leads to the Hole. The sign says, "Go directly to the Hole! Do not pass Go! Do not collect $200!" In effect it says, "Do not find a positive alternative that will strengthen your love!"

Beware! This way of viewing upsets is a product of our past training. We learned it when we learned to walk and talk. It is familiar in origin, passed on from our family of origin.

We saw that upsets, differences and challenges led to reactions. We learned how to react in various circumstances—to find the blame, to criticize the other person, to blow up, to defend ourselves, or to shut down when upset occurs.

Different partners may specialize in various tactics and skills, but we all tend to think that upsets are "bad."

This is a road sign that points straight to the Hole.

ENVISION A NEW PATH

If you want to travel on a new road, you need to set your sights on it. In other words, you will have to set a conscious intention for where you want to go.

Should you just drift along unconsciously, until the next relationship problem or issue pushes you into the Hole? Or do you want to go in a different direction?

You can travel on a new road—if you want.

But you have to consciously set your mind on the path you will take. Specifically, you need to clearly set your intentions and change how you view relationship challenges.

To be effective, your intention needs to serve as your core basis for understanding—in a new, constructive way—what is going on when upsets or challenges arise.

Take an example from sports. If an athlete lets each upset take him to the Hole, he might end up dropping out of the game—or worse, stop playing the sport. But if he sees it as an opportunity to improve his strategy, he will do that instead.

Or apply this to career development. If you run into a big hurdle, will it serve you to blame others, or find fault with the field you are in? Or will it be more useful to see you have an opportunity to learn new, vital skills?

Why would relationships be any different?

So here is a useful point of view...

It means that "**AN OPPORTUNITY FOR PERSONAL GROWTH IS AT HAND**"

This is okay... a positive sign...
you can work with it...

If a relationship upset or challenge comes up, it means you have an important opportunity for *personal growth*.

For instance, a past wound may have been triggered and is now coming up for healing. Or maybe an old unconscious pattern is running you—and you can now finally learn to see it and expand beyond it.

These are all positive things. They give you a new road to travel—a road that's all about "Growth."

This way of viewing Challenges leads you to... Expand your map and take a new road!

Viewing upsets or challenges as opportunities for personal growth opens a new road up for you. Setting your intention to grow puts you on that positive path.

Setting a conscious intention is the single most important factor in relating. It has a power that goes far beyond the communication techniques, like active listening, you might be taught in typical counseling sessions.

All those techniques usually go out the window, if you see upsets in the usual way. But if you commit yourself to a conscious intention like personal growth, this new viewpoint will provide a new framework for positive results.

Seeing opportunities for growth becomes the lens through which you view and understand the meaning of all events that take place. Holding this viewpoint will direct the manner in which you'll respond—or react—to each event.

Like the perception of the guy who crashed through the line at the movies, your viewpoint supplies the meaning of what just happened. One vision was that the guy was blind, doing the best he could. The other was that he was trying to upset people in line. You will react according to the perception you have of the event, as in this story:

The only survivor of a shipwreck was washed up on a small, uninhabited island. Every day he anxiously scanned the horizon for help, but none was forthcoming. Exhausted, he eventually managed to build a little hut out of driftwood to protect himself from the elements, and to store the few valuables he had been able to take from the wreck.

But then one day, after scavenging for food, he arrived home to find his little hut in flames, the smoke rolling up to the sky. The worst had happened—everything was lost! He was stunned with grief and anger, ready to end it all.

Early the next day, he was awakened by the sound of a ship that was approaching the island. It had come to rescue him. "How did you know I was here?" asked the weary man of his rescuers. "We saw your smoke signal," they replied.

Remember, the next time your hut seems to be on fire—it just may be a smoke signal that will save you.

In a relationship, your viewpoint affects how you react to events. Usually, when the event is that you are getting upset— all bets are off! The familiar viewpoint we bring to relationship is that upset is a sign that something is wrong. So we react by going to the Hole.

For a conscious intention to empower us, it must provide an understanding that will inspire us to face challenges in a new and positive way.

"Growth" is one such higher intention. It says that a relationship challenge is actually an opportunity for personal growth. That happens to be the truth, by the way.

SET A CONSCIOUS INTENTION

Setting your intention will be powerful to the extent that it truly taps into your highest aspirations and even spiritual perspective. It provides the answer to the question, "What am I really here to do in life, anyway?"

The unconscious viewpoint most of us coast along with gives a superficial answer—"We're here to have fun and be happy, or blame each other if we aren't."

Being upset or challenged is not a part of that viewpoint. It is seen as an obstacle to the goal. Therefore, when upsets and challenges come along, we have no guiding light to point towards any positive result.

There's an old Japanese saying:

"The obstacle is the path."

This is an example of viewing challenges in a way that can

lead to positive results. Every relationship includes challenges. Our unconscious, familiar viewpoint does not point us anywhere useful, just to the Hole. It does not take us to the paradise we briefly glimpsed in the honeymoon.

Normally, couples in the honeymoon think "This is it!" Anything that follows, where upsets happen, is undesirable. The familiar state of relationship, after the honeymoon, is to lament the loss of the magic—and to resent the apparently unresolvable persistence of upsets and challenges.

We normally view upsets and challenges in that negative light. This disconnects us from our higher intentions. It also disables us from responding in a positive direction.

But upsets and challenges are inevitable.

If we truly want to go down a new and positive road, we need to set our intention and adopt a new attitude. We need to find a new way of seeing upsets and challenges—a view that points us to the positive opportunity in each challenge—a vision that brings our highest intentions to life.

It is said that if couples share a deep enough love, they will be able to face anything. Well, love is not enough. If you want lasting happiness, plan for the challenges. Make a resolution to turn each challenge into an opportunity for personal growth.

In this sense, know that your hut will occasionally be put to the test of fire. Open your eyes to see that challenges and upsets are inevitable. They are valuable opportunities to grow, heal and become whole. If you do this, your relationship will keep moving on a positive, rewarding path.

Setting a conscious intention will help you find your way through the darkness. It gives a new meaning to the currently popular phrase, "What you *see* is what you *get*."

YOUR HIGHEST INTENTIONS

Here are some of the conscious intentions that empower and uplift us:

- **Personal Growth**
- **Wholeness**
- **Freedom**
- **Healing**
- **Presence**
- **Balance**
- **Inner Peace**
- **Being Clear**
- **Self Realization**

The intentions on the list above point to higher aspirations. They reach out toward spiritual ideals.

Each of these are significant on a personal level. Growth is something we want in our lives as individuals. So is wholeness, freedom, healing, inner peace, self-realization, balance—and all the other things on the list.

The intention you set must be personally compelling. It is not something cooked up because it sounds nice. To be effective, it needs to tap into what is meaningful for you.

One way to explore your intention is to answer the question:

**"In the end, after all is said and done...
What am I really here to achieve in life?"**

A big question like that deserves a big answer.

You may already know which word—or words—above reach you on the deepest level of your soul. There may be a better word that says it for you.

Another way to explore it is to look into your past. Find a time when you overcame an obstacle. Perhaps it was in your career, in school, in sports, or some other part of your life that is meaningful to you.

It was difficult, but you persisted—despite getting upset at times. There may have been moments you did not know what to do, or how it would all turn out. But for the most part, you kept at it and applied yourself.

Overcoming it was a great achievement. There may have been direct rewards in the world—like getting the job done well, advancing to a better position, being recognized.

But beyond that, you achieved something on an inner level that you really feel good about as you look back. Look again at the list above and sense if any of the words capture it.

Yet another way to explore your higher intention is to take inventory of any baggage from your past—old wounds, ways you react, sensitivities, triggers or hot buttons. Think of what you have already overcome in life—or what still affects you and you want to get beyond.

Now look at the list of words again. See if there is an intention that captures your desire to overcome baggage.

You may find there is a set of words which best portray your true intentions. Or, depending on circumstances, one or another word might do it.

For instance, we have always liked the combination of "Personal Growth" and "Healing."

Another good one is "Freedom"—which for us takes on the meaning of expansion, and the release of old limits and self-made reasons for suffering.

Truth be told, all the words on the list are synonyms.

Now consider the applicability of holding your higher intention as a first priority in life. Even if you do not clearly know which word (or words) matches your higher intention, imagine the following.

Imagine you are fully committed to your true higher intention. Feel it growing within you. Now envision how it would support you to do the following:

- **You would embrace all challenges that may otherwise take you to the Hole.**
- **You would see these challenges in a new, positive light.**
- **You would stay focused on a truly meaningful higher inner goal.**
- **You would feel courage to face challenges.**
- **You would be more constructive rather than going into the Hole.**

A higher intention is an umbrella covering all things that can take you to the Hole. It helps you to bring your best to any situation—including challenges and upsets.

Some people believe an intention like "Healing" is great when it comes to emotions. They see how that goes back to childhood wounds that need healing. But when it comes to money issues, well that's something entirely different!

It's important that your intention embraces everything that normally takes you to the Hole. It covers issues about money, sex, power, childraising, picking a new car, whatever...

A higher intention will embrace any challenge. It helps you see it in a new, positive light. It will move you toward a meaningful higher goal. It will give you courage to face the challenge and be constructive instead of going to the Hole.

A FOUNDATION TO BUILD LOVE

Setting a conscious intention is like making a blueprint for a house. It's a plan for building a relationship—and a life. It gives a foundation on which you can be constructive. It guides your efforts to create something that will stand through time.

Many times, people I see had already been exposed to good techniques for building better communication, resolving conflict, and so forth. But techniques alone may not be sufficient and under stress we often forget to use them.

Techniques, no matter how great, are like knowing how to install a window, tile a countertop, or hook up electrical outlets. Alone, they do not tell you how to build a house. Your higher intention is the blueprint for the home you want to live in. It sets the foundation upon which you build your home.

More accurately, though, it involves you in a process. It is not just the destination. It's the sign that points down a new road to be actively travelled.

When your intention is "Growth," it reminds and supports you to engage in a process of personal growth whenever challenges or upsets arise. It's not about getting to the end of the road. It's about how to take your very next step.

Whenever upsets or challenges occur, we are always at a fork in the road. We can go to the Hole or we can take a new path. Remembering our higher intention supports us to move in the direction we truly want to travel.

COMMIT TO YOUR TRUE HIGHER INTENTIONS

Committing to your true higher intention will give you the strength to face and overcome challenges and obstacles to your happiness.

Most of us do not actively hold such an intention. Instead, we simply react to whatever is going on in our lives. This puts us on an unending merry-go-round in which our circumstances and situations determine how we feel and act.

Aligning yourself with a personal intention that embraces challenges as opportunities gives you strength. It helps you to keep moving in a positive direction in your life, regardless of the circumstances you encounter.

Seeing the "big picture" in any challenging situation gives you added motivation and energy to successfully face and overcome what challenges you. You stay more resourceful and able to find constructive options. You are better able to keep yourself from falling into the Hole of reactivity, where positive options disappear and you get stuck in negativity.

Whether or not you have a partner willing to explore their higher intention, do the following brief exercise—just for yourself. Doing it may be the single most important thing you can do to change the direction of your life.

Do this even if you already know your higher intention...

Look again at this list of words. Which words offer the most power to inspire you to face upsets and challenges?

- **Personal Growth**
- **Wholeness**
- **Freedom**
- **Healing**
- **Presence**
- **Balance**
- **Inner Peace**
- **Being Clear**
- **Self Realization**

Use each word above in the following sentence:

"I deeply know that each challenge in life is an opportunity to expand my _____. When I remember this it gives me strength to embrace a challenge and move forward."

What are your top three words?

Is there one word that seems to imply all the rest?

Take a moment now and choose the most powerful word— or set of words—that defines your highest intention.

If you have any uncertainty at this point as to what your intention is, we strongly recommend that you commit to the following vision:

Personal Growth, Wholeness & Healing

Next, write your intention on a small piece of paper, by filling in the spaces in the following sentences:

"**I commit myself to see each challenge as an important opportunity for** _____.
"**I commit to use any relationship problems or upsets in the service of** _____.
"**Whenever I find myself reacting, placing blame, judging others, getting defensive, shutting down, or acting out of my negative emotions, I commit to stop and see how the situation is asking me to move forward to** _____.
"**I commit to embrace all such challenges and upsets in the spirit of** _____."

Now fold up that piece of paper and put it in your wallet. Carry it with you at all times.

When do you take out that small paper and read it?

Take it out if you're in a situation that is challenging you. Take it out whenever you feel upset. Take it out if you are thinking negative thoughts about anyone, including yourself. Take it out and take it's message to heart.

Use it as a reminder to be proactive—not reactive.

BE PROACTIVE

Being proactive means showing up consciously.

In love, at first we coast along unconsciously in a purely receptive role. But after the honeymoon, we are called upon to show up in a more conscious, proactive way. We can't keep floating along in the receptive role and hope to continually be uplifted. Something needs to shift. We do.

After the honeymoon we will sometimes get upset, and draw each other into that upset. Then who is left to deliver the inspiring feelings of love? Nobody!

Seduced by the receptive phase of love and by the popular myths of "true love"—we unconsciously define our perfect partner as someone who uplifts us even when we are down.

So when the honeymoon is over, our feeling of being with our perfect life partner may also be put into doubt.

Perhaps you have already noticed that the popular myth of "true love" leaves out that old saying: "A good relationship requires work!"

This is not an insignificant omission.

Indeed, if we want turn the honeymoon into a lasting relationship, we need to bring it down to earth. We need to revise our own personal definition of true love to recognize that "ever after" includes feelings other than happiness.

There will be challenges. We will be required to do work. As the honeymoon ends, we shift out of the receptive phase of love. We enter the next phase, which asks us to be conscious, to be proactive, to show up in a new way.

Committing to a personal intention is a vital element of being proactive. Such an intention defines who we are, and who we will become.

Here's a saying to keep in mind: "A good relationship is no accident—it is intentional!"

Know where you want your love—and life—to go. Define this by the highest intention you keep alive. Consciously choose the path you want to be on.

PROBLEM OR OPPORTUNITY?

We can see relationship issues one way, or the other—as a problem or as an opportunity. We can't see both ways at once. So pick wisely the road you want to travel.

To make this practical, think of any minor issue you are experiencing—or have recently had—with anyone.

Don't come up with the most overwhelming relationship issue of your life. Pick something that is a 3 on a scale of 10 in terms of being upsetting to you.

As you think about this issue, answer these questions:

1. What's the problem? What's wrong?

2. How does this upset, limit or hurt you?

3. How will this ruin your future if it continues?

4. Whose fault is it?

The above questions are part of the "Blame Game." Notice what mood they put you in. Are they taking you anywhere you really want to go?

Some variation on these types of questions is how most of us tend to automatically think about things. We need to be very alert to how this process works inside our brains.

The idea of identifying a problem in order to fix it seems reasonable enough. But the trouble is that most of us get stuck in the problem identification to the point that we only end up blaming everyone else for how things are.

There is little room for growth or expansion of positive options in the "Blame Game."

Think of it as if you are going to a travel agency. Your last trip was to Detroit—and it did not work out very well for you. It was too crowded, too industrial, too much noise, the people were rude, and you had a terrible time.

(Detroit fans, I apologize: I'm making this all up!)

Anyway, the travel agent asks you where you want to go. He is poised at his keyboard to type in your destination.

You: "I hate Detroit. It is terrible there."

Agent: "Where did you say you want to go?"

You: "Detroit really is bad. People are so rude...."

Agent: "Right. But where do you want to go?"

You: "It's so crowded in Detroit, I can't understand why anyone would want to go there! So much pollution..."

Being in the "Blame Game" is like telling the travel agent where you don't want to go. Somehow, upset, you cannot seem to get around to specifying your real destination.

Focusing on an issue as a problem will keep you stuck. All you are talking about is what you do not want.

Just as the travel agent cannot make sense of where you do not want to go—your brain cannot make purposefully positive sense of negative statements.

Here's a simple experiment to prove this...

Do not think of a blue elephant.

So what is the first thing that came to your mind?

Of course, a blue elephant.

See how that works?

We need to treat our brain as our inner travel agent. Tell it where we do want to go. Say, "I want to go to Hawaii."

If you see relationship issues as positive opportunities, this helps your brain move you in a positive direction.

Here is a different set of questions. Think about the same relationship issue and answer these questions:

1. What do you want?

2. What will you see, hear and feel if you get it?

3. How might you go about getting it?

4. How can you use any obstacle as an opportunity to personally learn and grow?

These questions put you in the "Opportunity Frame." Notice what mood they put you in. Are they taking you to a new and more positive place?

Years ago, a reporter was interviewing Albert Einstein near the end of his life. He had already seen the fruits of his genius in the world, including the atom bomb. This young reporter was trying to draw out Einstein's wisdom.

He asked, "Dr. Einstein. What do you consider the most important question in the universe?"

Einstein pondered and answered that the most important question is, "How is the world a friendly place?"

To shift how you think about the world is to shift the world itself. You will empower yourself to get positive results when you set your intentions for where you truly want to go.

Ask the right question to yourself and move forward.

CHAPTER THREE

CLAIM YOUR OWN BAGGAGE

"If you want the present to be different from the past, study the past."—SPINOZA

**WELCOME TO THE
BAGGAGE CLAIM AREA**

PLEASE PROCEED WITH CARE:

**1. LOCATE EACH OF THE PIECES
2. IDENTIFY OWNERSHIP
3. OPEN & EXAMINE CONTENTS**

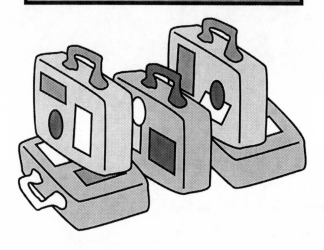

All travelers know about the Baggage Claim Area. We stand around impatiently and wait for our luggage to appear. There is usually a crowd of people competing to be at the front of the line. We are alert to spot our baggage, since it is filled with valuables. We wouldn't want anyone else to walk off with our stuff. Nor would we want to leave any of our bags behind.

In relationship, it is usually the exact opposite.

When our baggage shows up, we stand around denying it's our stuff. We pretend that everything that gets stacked up in the Baggage Claim Area belongs to our partner—not to us!

No, we don't own a single thing there among the stacks and stacks of unclaimed emotional baggage.

THE BAGGAGE CLAIM DISPUTE
Is it yours... or the other persons?

The big dispute in relationship often is: "Whose baggage is this?" Each partner is likely to say, "It's the other person's stuff that's causing the problem here."

Remember the fish in the bowl of water? We see the water the fish lives in—but to the fish itself, the water is invisible. Likewise, we see our partner's baggage, but we have a major blindspot for our own.

Thus we quite earnestly react as if our partner is the cause of the current issue. The typical statement about baggage is that it's the other person who has something wrong with them, and that is what causes the problem, upset or challenge. For instance:

- "What's your problem?"
- "Deal with it!"
- "Get off of it."
- "You act just like a little child!"
- "He needs to get his act together!"
- "She never lets up... she's so insecure."
- "He's so insensitive and walled-off."

We focus on baggage that is apparently held by the other person. They need to get their act together, deal with their problems or personality deficits. They need to change so we can feel better. All of us have a huge blind spot for the part we play in a situation, the emotional baggage we carry, and our own 95% factor.

THE VIEW FROM CHILDHOOD

- The other person is big and powerful
- Wounds come from that big person
- Needs met or not by that big person

Looking at the other person as the source of upset is built into the baggage itself. Baggage is just another name for the 95% factor, discussed above with the map from the past. This originated in childhood, when "family" created "familiar" behaviors and feelings.

Childhood was a time when the other person, namely our parent, *was* larger than us and more powerful. They were the source of love and nourishment, and the means by which our needs were met—or neglected.

Our childhood experience made the other person the apparent source and cause of our pleasure or pain. When we were emotionally hurt as children, whether our parents intended it or not, they were causally linked to the wound.

We gradually came to certain conclusions about the world. We learned our particular emotional coping strategies, what to react to—and how to express or suppress our feelings.

In childhood, we literally figured out what to hook up our "fight or flight" reaction to—what will trigger us to feel fear, pain or anger. We developed our own particular way of acting when we get upset—whether that is to fight, to go into flight, or to freeze.

Any event today that is even slightly similar to a past wound tends to bring up the energy of that earlier wound. This amplifies our emotional reaction to the current event. Linked to this emotional amplification is the sense of a larger, more powerful person as the source of it.

This process of emotional amplification is unconscious, so we may not even recognize that it is going on. What we do recognize is that we are getting upset. This becomes the apparent problem for us. What is happening is the 95% factor is kicking in, coming up out of the map of our past.

Most of our emotional triggers, hot buttons, sensitivities, wounds, patterns and limiting beliefs remain linked to the sense of a larger, more powerful other person. We sense that other person makes us feel upset.

Sentences like "You make me angry!" or "You drive me crazy!" seem to be part of the syntax of love. We say them easily—and question them rarely.

By the time we are adults in relationship, we have a fully developed map for what causes our feelings. The cause is almost always seen as being external to ourselves. We do not recognize how our baggage is involved. It clearly looks to us as if the other person makes us feel the way we do.

It is a fact that we all have blind spots about the real source of our emotional reactions. We are not consciously choosing to feel upset, certainly. But this does not mean the other person is making us feel the way we do.

Quite the contrary. We merely do not see—or own—the actual inner source of our suffering.

In challenging circumstances, it is essential to question what we are *not* seeing. Especially within ourselves. It even pays to question the basic validity of thinking in terms of cause and effect. This kind of thinking keeps us from recognizing the larger picture—in which we play an integral part in the events of our lives.

We give up our power when we believe we have no role in things. It is time to question our basic assumptions.

Unconsciously, we believe every feeling we have has an external cause, some outside person or event making us upset. We think we can't help what we feel or do when we feel it. We are simply a puppet pulled by strings.

This is an erroneous, self-limiting belief.

It's like someone who has never seen a cat. This person is

looking through a narrow slit in a fence, and, on the other side, a cat walks by. He sees first the head, then later the tail.

He reasons the head is the cause of the tail. This absurd idea is a failure to see that head and tail go together.

As Alan Watts[1] said, it is all one cat. The cat wasn't born as a head which, some time later, caused a tail. It was born whole, one entire cat. Our observer's mistake was looking through a narrow slit. He couldn't see the whole cat at once.

THEY MAKE US FEEL THE WAY WE DO

When we think our partner "causes" our feelings, we fail to see our actual role in the relationship we are co-creating. We also fail to see that probably 95% of the upsets we feel inside of us has nothing to do with our partner.

We do this quite unconsciously. We unconsciously transfer the causality of all our feelings to our current partner. In the honeymoon, they make us feel great. Then later, they upset us. We need them to change so we can feel better again.

I often ask people to close their eyes and get a quick image or sense of their partner, who is apparently causing their upset feelings. Then I inquire whether they sense their partner is larger, the same size or smaller than they are.

Usually they sense the other person large and themselves as small. I then ask them, "When was the last time in their life that was really the case?"

Of course, it was when they were children.

Couples are often startled to recognize how deeply ingrained the tendency is to assign an external blame to their upsets. We like to think it is the other person who makes us feel what we do, and that they are the ones who can and should change how we feel.

You know the 95% factor has kicked in and you are headed for the Hole, when the source of your upset appears to be the other person—and you believe that only they can help you feel better, if they would only change.

In this condition, we totally disown any adult responsibility for our feelings. We collapse into a childlike state of thinking our partner has total control over our emotional state.

SIGNS OF BEING IN A "CHILDLIKE" STATE

- Wanting them to change
- Believing they "made" us upset
- Thinking it's 100% about them... Not us
- Not seeing the emotional affect of our past

We want them to change. We blame them for how we feel. We think that whatever feelings are coming up for us here and now are 100% a product of what they are doing.

It's like we put our partner into a movie of childhood, casting them in the role of one of our parents. Then we act out our part in the movie and treat them accordingly.

Recall again the example of Sarah and Michael and his failed attempt to lighten things up by teasing her. She blew up, called him insensitive, and they ended up in the Hole.

Unconsciously, she cast him in the role of her father who teased her abusively as a child. At the moment her 95% factor kicked in she experienced rage in her body. She identified Michael as the sole cause—the only blame for her upset feelings. She verbally reacted to him accordingly.

But Sarah did not recognize that her own past baggage was involved. She did not remember her father. Nor did she sense how wounds from her past amplified her emotions like a amplifier, accelerating her ride to the Hole.

We need to claim our baggage from the past and take an active role in healing it—otherwise it will unconsciously block us from the love we truly want.

Far from disclaiming old baggage or thinking that our reactions are caused by a partner, look for your own part in an upset. Know that this will be a route to healing the old wounds and self-limits which otherwise get carried throughout life.

Like Susan finally realized one day, recognize the power of looking within. Think of it this way: "if nobody pushes my buttons, then how will I ever grow and heal?"

You reclaim your power and grow when you finally own the active part you play in a relationship. If you pretend that problems are all the other person's fault, you remain powerless, keeping all your baggage. Even if you were to move to another relationship, that same baggage will accompany you.

Erica, another client, told in her initial session that she was now in her third significant relationship. She had been married twice and was now with a long term lover.

In her first marriage there were so many problems that she eventually divorced him. Her second marriage had similar problems to the ones she experienced in the first marriage and so she ended up divorcing him, as well.

At that point, Erica concluded that the real problem was men, per se. She decided that it was impossible to have a good relationship with a man. So she decided that her next partner would be a woman.

She had been with Maria for three years now. To her great surprise, the very same problems came up!

Contemplating this turn of events, Erica realized there was only one common factor in all three relationships—and that factor was *her*.

Realizing this, she decided to look at whatever was in her that resulted in the unhappiness of each relationship. She started this personal growth by taking stock of the emotional baggage and reactivity she carried into each relationship.

TAKE STOCK OF YOUR REACTIONS

If you are willing to look at your own baggage, you are half way to emotional freedom. This isn't about becoming the "blame" for everything gone wrong. It is about seeing your reaction patterns—so you can expand beyond them. This will help you to free yourself from inner suffering and unconscious childlike emotional behaviors.

The chart on the next page helps you take stock of your own emotional patterns. You will analyze how you tend to get upset—and how you behave when you are upset.

The chart explores four types of reactions: anger, fear, sadness and confusion. Within each type of upset, there are different words that may make more sense to you. Irritation, for instance, appears with anger, because it is a form of anger. Similarly, insecurity is a form of fear.

Note the frequency you have feelings in each of these four types—often, sometimes or seldom. Then put in how you express the feeling. How do you show it, or keep it inside?

Take anger, for instance. Maybe you feel it as frustration. Do you express this by yelling, criticism, crying, sarcasm? Or do you suppress it, withdraw, numb out, ruminate over it, stew in silent resentment?

FEELING (Reaction)	How often do you feel it?	How do you express this feeling?
Anger Irritation Frustration	often sometimes seldom	
Fear Anxiety Insecurity	often sometimes seldom	
Sadness Hurt Grief	often sometimes seldom	
Confusion Numb Blank	often sometimes seldom	

Notice if there are certain feelings you tend to feel often. Equally important, are there any you seldom feel?

Treat this information as data. Ask yourself if you have access to all feeling states. Look at whether you express the feelings you have in a way that you ideally would want to, in an adult way representing you at your best.

Now it's time to ask some hard questions:

Are there any emotional reactions you tend to have, more childlike in nature?

Take anger. It could be quite obvious that acting out anger by having a fit is childlike. But what about holding it in? What about avoiding conflict? That may appear more adult, but is it really? Or is there a childlike element to it, underneath?

If you are big enough to see and admit you do have some childlike reactive patterns—what do these cost you? Are they getting you the loving relationship you truly want? Can you start to envision a more mature you, dealing with these inner feelings in a more responsible and adult manner?

TAKE STOCK OF YOUR COPING STRATEGIES

In relationship, you are not the only person who gets upset. It's time to take stock of how you tend to cope when your partner expresses upset. It may be any kind of upset—anger, hurt, anxiety. It may be any way they behave—pursue you, withdraw, cry, criticize, blow up, stonewall, get defensive.

The following chart lists coping strategies.

Put a check by strategies you use if your partner is upset. For common ones, make a note of the specific behavior your partner does that gets you to use that coping strategy.

Your Coping Strategy	Your Partner's Behavior
Use logic, reason with them	
Intellectualize	
Defend yourself	
Argue the point, correct them	
Counter-blame them	
Ridicule	
Make a joke of it	
Ignore or avoid the situation	
Distance, leave, withdraw	
Get confused	
Go numb, freeze up, dissociate	
Judge them	
Label them, criticize, name call	
Be right, make them wrong	
React with fear, anger, hurt	
Take on their feelings	
Support their victim stance	
See yourself as victim	
Take care of their feelings	
Try to change their feelings	
Distract them	
Feel guilty	
Feel responsible for their upset	

Would it surprise you that the coping strategies above are childlike? They don't lead to great results. When you use them, you are not acting at your best.

Again, this is not about taking on the role of being the "blame" for how things go wrong in your relationships. There is no positive use to assigning that role to anyone.

We take honest stock of ourselves in order to start seeing what is normally in our blind spot. If it stays in our blind spot, we can run into it without even knowing it.

What are we blind to? The thing we tend not to see in our relationships is our own patterns. We miss seeing how our own thoughts, feelings and actions are affecting the state of things. Our eyes are usually looking outside ourselves.

We are experts at scoping out the other person. We know exactly what their hangups are—and how they need to grow and mature for things to be better. We know exactly how they need to change to make us feel better.

This leaves us totally blind to ourselves, and the actual impact we are having on others.

We only look through the narrow slit in the fence at what the other person does, and put that together with how we feel. The cat's head does not "cause" its tail. What our partner does is not the "cause" of our feelings.

We are directly involved in how our relationship unfolds. Even taking a passive stance has an affect, and gets a negative result for us. This is called passive aggression.

As they say, even not communicating is communicating.

Instead of looking at your relationship through a slit in the fence—see it as a mirror of yourself.

Your relationship issues are giving you continual feedback on parts of you that may need to grow.

See how you are thinking about your situation.

Notice any limiting beliefs you have.

Examine how you tend to react to things.

They say that 5% of life is what happens; the other 95% is how we react to it. Growth involves updating our beliefs and unconscious tendencies to react.

We learn the bulk of our reaction patterns by eight years old. By then, we have formed our core beliefs about the world around us—and how we should react to it.

Next we will look more systematically at how this gets put together and forms a part of our personalities. We will explore this in the spirit of personal growth, of seeing more clearly the new road you may want to take.

CHAPTER FOUR

RECOGNIZE THE BOX YOU ARE IN

"Every person mistakes the limits of their own field of vision for the limits of the world."—SCHOPENHAUER

Our emotional stressors, coping strategies, and related past baggage is part of our personality structure. It is a kind of box we are in. It limits our happiness in love. To get out of this box, we first need to see it. Then we can begin to grow.

Between the ages of two and eight, we came to certain conclusions about the world, how to get along in it, how to react to it. We were affected by our family and friends, by our environment and various events.

This gave rise to our personality. Our personality exhibits many positive strengths, traits and abilities.

On the other hand, it also carries a specific pattern of self-limiting beliefs, emotional reactions, coping strategies, sensitivities, and counterproductive ways of acting. These are what damage our relationships—and block us from sustaining longterm satisfaction with each other.

People have different personalities. How many different types are there? What are they? How exactly does our type affect our ability to sustain happiness in a relationship?

Helen Palmer[3] and David Daniels[4], foundational teachers of the Enneagram personality system—describe nine basic personality archetypes.

At first, I did not like the idea I had one of the Enneagram personality types. It felt like I was being put into a box.

But then I realized that I was, in fact, already in a box.

We all repeat patterns that keep us from achieving the happiness we want in love. So I decided to examine the box I was in—with the intention to get out of it.

This attitude helps us to see our own unconscious patterns and overcome them. It helps us to work with differences—and to move beyond limiting beliefs and emotional obstacles.

Below, you will see each of the nine personality types.

You will see what is stressful to each type in relationships. You will see how each type tries to cope with stress—and the resulting relationship problems that arise for that type due to their particular style of coping.

For each type you will discover the underlying core beliefs developed in childhood. These beliefs are an unseen force that deeply affect us. They are at the root of the baggage we carry, giving rise to our emotional reactions and behaviors.

The core beliefs paint the world a different color for each personality type. They lead each type to experience predictable problems in a relationship.

Until we see and overcome the effects of our own limiting beliefs and coping strategies, we will continue to react in ways that cause us more stress, and damage our relationships.

We all carry old beliefs and baggage that block us. We must all look within ourselves to overcome the limits of our subconscious beliefs and coping strategies.

In the following sketches you will see how each type can engage in personal growth.

Don't worry if you cannot figure out your type. Get a sense of what applies to you, and especially look for anything that points you towards your own personal growth.

Type 1: The Perfectionist

A Perfectionist is concerned with being good, correcting error, doing what one should, and getting things right.

They have an active inner voice that guides them to do the right thing. But this inner voice is critical and overbearing, and it tends to produce inner tension, guilt, and worry. In its wake, pleasure gets dampened. Personal needs are not recognized or voiced. A sense of deprivation can result.

The dominant focus on what is "good" and "right" gets put out into relationships. The strong sense of "it should be this way" voiced by the Perfectionist—in the interest of what seems right—makes it look like there's only one way of doing things, their way. The other person generally does not like this, and may end up feeling like they are walking on egg-shells. In their "rightness" the Perfectionist seems to be superior—while the other person feels picked apart, rejected, hurt, inferior.

There is a tendency to be overly black and white about things. This creates stress and a sense of trying to be in control. It also reduces happiness. People in relationship with a Perfectionist often wish things could just be more relaxed and easy. They yearn for a more flexible approach to things.

Personal growth for a Perfectionist is to internally ask the question: "Would I rather be right—or happy?" It will help to see and question what seem to be rigid rules. Learn to accept mistakes. Recognize that there are different ways of doing things besides the one "right" way. Two great virtues for a Perfectionist to develop are patience and compassion. True serenity is gained by accepting things as they are, even what appear to be "imperfections."

Type 2: The Giver

A Giver is focused on fulfilling other peoples' needs. They believe they'll get love and connection in this way.

They usually give too much. But they seldom ask for what they want or need. So they get back too little—since others do not have a Giver's "psychic" ability to see needs. Eventually they break into anger, or just as easily, tears. They, and their partners, get overwhelmed by these emotional outbreaks.

A Giver puts so much energy into gaining connection by giving, that other people see this as too much, out of balance, possibly even manipulative. So others retreat—as the Giver pursues them. Under these conditions, a Giver can be viewed as overly needy or too dependent.

Most relationships encounter discrepancies between one partner wanting to be closer, and the other wanting space. The Giver usually suffers the lack of connection in this classic "connection vs. space" dance. This leaves them particularly vulnerable to feeling rejected and the pain of loss. Their pursuit of connection often will push the other person to need even more space. This polarization process results in both partners suffering.

Personal growth for a Giver is to scale back their strong drive for giving—and reduce their dependency on connecting. Know that love does not depend on altering oneself to fit the needs of others. A Giver will grow if they practice setting boundaries and saying "no." By spending time alone, they learn to better sense their own needs—and how to fulfill these needs, themselves. A Giver also grows as they begin to directly ask others for what they want.

Type 3: The Performer

A Performer is concerned with work and getting the job done. They are driven by the need to succeed. In essence, they believe that love and acceptance is based upon what they do, on their performance, image, achievements and success. With their high drive to get the job done, a Performer often puts feelings aside—their feelings as well as the feelings of other people. This becomes a problem in relationships.

For the Performer, accomplishments are seen to be the measure of a person's worth. This leaves them very dependent on external approval and recognition, based on how well they succeed in accomplishing things.

In relationship, others may sense they are not cared for, especially because their feelings are ignored by the Performer. The whole realm of emotional contact will seem to be missing. People want to know what a Performer feels. But there is discomfort around the arena of emotions, so a Performer will avoid this vital area of human interchange. Their partners end up feeling a lack of connection. As a Performer gets stuck in to-do lists and workaholism, their emotional absence will become the critical issue.

Personal growth for a Performer is to know and honor their feelings, and to freely discuss feelings with others. They grow with the realizion they are a human beings, not human "doings." They also need to become the source of their own acceptance and appreciation, rather than depending on external recognition. It is vital for a Performer to slow down and smell the roses—to feel good while doing nothing—and appreciate the importance of emotion in life and love.

Type 4: The Romantic

A Romantic is an idealist who longs for a special sense of connection in the world. They are often disappointed by life. They feel something important is missing. They tend to be dissatisfied or angry with ordinary, daily life. They yearn for that special something believed to be ultimately fulfilling.

Relationships are concerned with a search for the special and unique. Romantics suffer from a "grass is always greener" syndrome. They are attracted by distance and non-availability. But once things settle down, they get bored or start to see what is missing or not good enough in the other person. Hence, they have trouble committing. Lasting happiness is elusive.

A Romantic perennially longs for a depth and intensity of emotional connection. Yet it always seems missing, and their partner fails to match their idealized yearnings.

They feel special, different, but at times they also feel like a misfit. They seem to generate dramatic crises, easily feeling rejected, abandoned, jealous, or envious. They can become subject to having huge emotional swings. People have difficulty coping with their intense drama. Others can also feel rejected, as being seen as not good enough.

Personal growth for a Romantic is to see what is positive in life in the moment, rather than what is missing. Learn to enjoy being in the "here and now." Find things to appreciate in ordinary everyday experiences. Growth occurs as a Romantic maintains a consistent course of action, despite intense mood swings. They need to slow down and delay their emotional reactions. Additionally, helping others is good for a Romantic, offering a way to become less self-absorbed.

Type 5: The Observer

An Observer tends to think the world demands too much, and gives too little. They focus on protecting themselves from intrusions or demands made on them by others. They value privacy. They need signficant amounts of time alone. They will tend to be detached and will easily withdraw from others. Emotional states overwhelm an Observer—both their own feelings and those of other people. Hence they will isolate from their feelings and try to avoid the feelings of the people around them. They retreat to the domain of the mind and intellect. Others find this void of emotional connection a kind of rejection, a sign their feelings don't matter.

The detached stance of an Observer can leave them feeling isolated. Lots of alone time may also bring with it the pain of feeling lonely. They may then long for connection. Yet at the same time, an Observer feels inadequate when it comes to connecting and dealing with real emotional interchange in relationships.

In the dance of "connection vs. space" they tend to need lots of space and can easily feel trapped. Others perceive them as unavailable, aloof, and try to get them to open up and talk about their feelings. It's easy to mistake an Observer's need for privacy as a form of rejection. Their retreat into the intellect can easily be seen as being superior.

Personal growth for an Observer is to become comfortable with feelings. Start sensing what you feel. And reveal this to others, in real time, as soon as you feel it. When you feel like withdrawing, move closer. Participate in life more, engage in conversation and discuss personal things about yourself.

Type 6: The Loyal Skeptic

A Loyal Skeptic is concerned with finding certainty or security. Their sense of being safe is challenged by a world that appears to be dangerous. This may take them in one of two directions—to fear the world, or to deny there is anything to fear. They may then believe you must avoid and escape—or face and fight—perceived danger.

A Loyal Skeptic is vigilant. They also tend to have many doubts, and can be highly ambivalent. They can easily misread or mistrust others. There can be difficulties with authority figures—either in the form of excess loyalty and obedience, or rebellion and opposition.

Danger can be seen everywhere. This can result in anxiety and fear—and increased vigilance. The Loyal Skeptic may focus excessively on negative future outcomes, the downside and what could go wrong. Trying to protect themselves from these imagined disasters, they will end up acting in ways that create self-fulfilling prophecies.

Others may feel a sense of being scrutinized, pursued or accused—often erroneously. People can be pushed away by the excessive vigilance and attempt to control them. Others resent that the Loyal Skeptic is projecting negative things onto them, and they yearn for a more relaxed state.

Personal growth for a Loyal Skeptic is to learn to embrace uncertainty. Begin to focus on the positive aspects of life, the positive qualities in other people. The ability to trust will be helped by internally asking the question "What if what I think I see here is not real?"—and then doing calm, respectful reality-testing with others.

Type 7: The Epicure

An Epicure is sensitive to how the world is limiting. They are frustrated with this, and try to keep as many options available as possible, to avoid limits or pain.

They are the ultimate pleasure seekers. They continually focus on pleasurable activities, and enjoy imagining all the many fascinating possibilities that could exist in the future. This becomes a major source of distraction, a diversion from deeper purposes and commitments.

An Epicure is a master at reframing negatives as positives. There is always a silver lining to every cloud. They are driven to focus on the lining, and avoid the cloud altogether. Trying to keep feeling happy, and trying to escape limits or pain, will actually lead to real losses in life. This will especially be true in relationships, and this will cause real pain.

In the "connection vs. space" dance in relationships, an Epicure will usually be the one who feels trapped and will need more space. They will usually have problems with committing to a relationship.

Others will react to an Epicure's avoidance of negative feelings. They may feel rejected or come to believe an Epicure really doesn't care about them. In trying to avoid or escape pain, an Epicure will fail to learn the deeper lessons that pain teaches us, and they will repeat the same mistakes.

Personal growth for an Epicure is to realize what the hunger for options and escape of pain actually costs. Accept limits. Learn to stay with one thing and overcome the feeling of being trapped and needing to escape. Embrace the here and now, whether painful or pleasurable, stimulating or boring.

Type 8: The Leader

A Leader tends to see the world as a hard place, where one has to be powerful or forceful. It's all about being protected and respected. Underlying this, a sense of innocence has been lost because the world appears harsh and unjust.

This results in a great concern with being in control of a situation. This can result in conflicts, struggles over power, and the Leader easily erupts into anger.

There are many different reactions to a Leader. Some people counter their force by fighting back. Many others simply withdraw or avoid them. The Leader then feels unmet or disrespected, resulting in more anger and struggle.

A Leader has the internal mandate to deny any fear or vulnerability. They tend towards excess and impulsive action. While most people would say "ready, aim, fire"—they will say "ready, fire, and who needs to aim?" Hence, they readily leap before they look, and overdo things. This can result in being exhausted, and rejected.

People often feel intimidated or intruded upon by a Leader. They are pushed away by the sense that, according to the Leader, "It's my way, or the highway." In relationships, others will feel a lack of the qualities of being soft, tender and sensitive—which in their need to deny vulnerability, a Leader hides even from themselves.

Personal growth for a Leader is to be more aware of their intense drive and energy, and to better manage their impulses. They grow as they realize true strength is in the ability to be receptive and open to others—and as they recover a natural sense of innocence, and acceptance of being vulnerable.

Type 9: The Peacemaker

A Peacemaker tends to "go along to get along." They put their needs and opinions on hold, and will blend into or merge with what other people want. In this way, they try to gain love, acceptance and a sense of belonging.

They often suffer from losing themselves in the more assertive agendas of others. They will rarely look inside themselves to see what they want. Hence they will seldom voice to others what they feel or need.

A Peacemaker will too quickly agree to things or go along with others' agendas, yet later end up resenting it, or resisting it. This makes other people angry. And anger presents a serious problem for a Peacemaker. They avoid feeling it. They avoid conflict. Instead, they numb out or fuzz out.

In relationship, others have problems with a Peacemaker not expressing feelings or needs—and with their difficulty in making timely decisions. People want the Peacemaker to say what they feel, and to more quickly say what they want.

A Peacemaker is overly focused on comfort. The excessive need for comfort means they avoid all possible conflict. They do not say what they want, because others might reject them, or it may lead to conflict. This leaves them unaware or non-assertive about their personal needs and agendas.

Personal growth for a Peacemaker is to know they are important. They need to know what they feel and want—and voice it to others. Learn to be more comfortable with conflict. Set better personal boundaries, even learn to say "no"—as this helps a Peacemaker better express their authentic self, and "show up" more in a relationship.

PERSONAL GROWTH IS THE KEY

Don't fret if you can't determine your personality type.

Just write down all suggestions for personal growth suggested for any type that seem to apply to you. Put these on a piece of paper. Look at this paper often. It holds what you will tend to overlook.

Doing what is on it is critical to your happiness.

I've seen many different combinations of types. Each pair suffers predictable issues. To effectively overcome core issues, we each must see the subconscious patterns our type brings into a relationship. The key to a great relationship is for us to recognize our own limiting patterns, and do the growth work to get out of the box we personally are in.

There is no one-size-fits-all solution for relationship issues. What you personally need to do depends on your own personality type, on the personal limits you need to face and overcome.

For one type, that may be to reduce emotional reactivity. For another, it may be to better voice and express feelings. For one, it may be to become more comfortable with distance. Yet for another, it may be to learn to better connect.

Whatever your path of growth is, if you simply act out the patterns of your personality type, you will bring predictable baggage into your relationships. To create positive changes, we each need to grow emotionally, expand beyond our ways of reacting—and enact new behaviors.

Relationship issues are often based on the differences between partners. Differences get magnified over time.

Another name for this is polarization.

CHAPTER FIVE

STOP THE POLARITY DANCE

*"Opposition brings concord. Out of discord comes
the fairest harmony."*—HERACLITUS

All couples tend to polarize over their differences. This is
a subconscious process. We are normally not aware of it
happening, until it gets very upsetting. Then it turns into a full
scale battle over who needs to change.

I call this destructive pattern a "polarity dance."

A polarity dance can suck happiness out of love. It is a
dance of *opposition*. Each partner puts down the opposite foot.
If one puts down their right, the other puts down their left.

Couples often move into opposition as they attempt to deal
with important differences. Most of us don't realize how easily
we do this. It's automatic and unconscious.

The polarity dance moves us straight to the Hole.

We need to go beyond a polarity dance to get to happier,
healthier relating. Below we will explore several of the popular
polarity dances that couples commonly do.

VARIOUS POLARITY DANCES

- **Connection vs. Space**
- **Closeness vs. Distance**
- **"Needy" vs. "Cold"**

One of the most difficult issues in relating is what happens
when we shift between *closeness* and *distance*.

In one way or another, most couples do this polarity dance.

It can happen whenever one person seems to be chasing the other for closeness or a stronger sense of connection—while the other person feels the need to distance.

A place where this can occur is around commitment. One partner may be dragging their feet, as the other puts on more pressure. Another place his happens is when one person strongly needs to know what the other is feeling, and the other person feels pressured, blanks out or backs away.

There are countless other places in a relationship that this unhappy but common dance might arise.

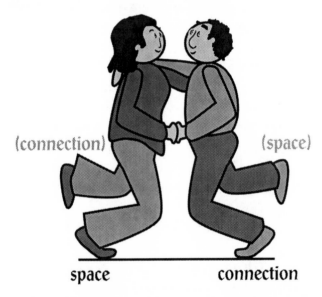

In this polarity dance, each partner puts down a different foot. One foot stands for connection and closeness. The other stands for distance and having your own space. In dancing the polarity, one partner wants distance, the other needs closeness. One wants connection, the other needs space.

As the polarity dance increases, it can bring up a feeling of abandonment in the partner who wants closeness. It can result in a feeling of overwhelm or entrapment in the partner who needs distance. These feelings are amplified by the 95% factor and past baggage carried around since childhood.

Take the example of Jim and Ann. Their relationship of ten years was in danger of ending. Jim complained that Ann didn't spend time with him, broke agreements to be together, and that she put more time and energy into her business than she put into the relationship. Ann complained that Jim was needy and insecure. She had to run a business and didn't have time to be with him every time he called.

Over a period of six weeks, we explored their past and how it was influencing them now. We discovered that beliefs and baggage developed in childhood were contaminating their relationship. Their childhood wounds were complementary. Jim had been abandoned as a child and still carried much anxiety and fear. Ann had been overly protected, with her personal privacy often violated by her parents.

They ended up developing quite different personality types—with different tendencies and reactions when it came to closeness and distance. After coming to better understand themselves and each other, they began to support each others' growth and healing. Each wanted to expand beyond their old patterns and learn new behaviors.

Jim learned how to give Ann space and soothe his own anxiety about this. In turn, she learned how to be present and stay with Jim, even though her old reaction was to leave in order to get space and reduce her anxiety.

Jim and Ann learned new skills, healed old wounds and

rekindled their love. They "popped" their polarity. The issue of closeness and distance lost its charge and they were able to find mutually satisfactory solutions for scheduling their time together and apart.

In the polarity dance, each partner keeps one foot on the ground. Their other foot is "in the air," or disowned. In reality, everyone needs connection and everyone needs space. A healthy relationship balances both needs. We each have two feet—and we need to use both to be whole.

But in the polarity dance, we pretend to have only one foot, the opposite of our partner's. We look down at our partner's foot as wrong. If they stand on their closeness foot, we may call them "needy" or "insecure." If they stand on their distance foot, we may call them "selfish" or "cold."

By doing this, we create even more pain and push each other to further extremes of opposition. We trigger each other's basic wounds around abandonment or entrapment, in deeper and deeper waves of upset and confusion.

The dance can suddenly reverse, and each partner puts down their opposite foot. Usually the partner pursuing closeness will back off and then the formerly distant partner starts feeling abandoned. They switch roles, trade places—but the pain does not stop.

Couples who develop happiness in relationship finally realize what's going on, and are willing to explore new options. Each person is willing to learn a better sense of balance between their own two feet. In that way, a couple can truly share closeness at times. And at other times, they can enjoy their own space. Both the "me" and the "we" can be nurtured— without friction or threat to the relationship.

• Avoidant vs. Volatile
• Held-Back vs. Explosive

Some personality types are avoidant in certain arenas of relating. Other types can be volatile to some degree or another. Both of these are reaction patterns to the presence of emotional energy. Either can damage a relationship.

Some people avoid all strong feelings. Others avoid certain feelings—like pain, anger, or fear. Avoidance sets up major limits in relating when such feelings come up.

Ironically, the more one tends to avoid, the more the very thing one is avoiding shows up. An example is someone who avoids anger, tries to be nice and please everyone. They somehow end up generating a lot of anger around them. This is because in all that avoiding, they never really show up in ways they are needed and wanted.

Even when both partners prefer to be avoidant, this can sap the juice right out of a relationship. Energy is kept low due to the fear of boat rocking. So while anger and upset are minimized, so is the energy crucial for passion.

Couples may proudly say "we never fight." But there is a high cost for staying inside the comfort zone—even if both people agree to the avoidant strategy.

Volatility is a different way of coping with strong feelings. In actuality, a volatile person has no better skill at dealing with emotional energy than an avoidant type. Instead of stuffing their energy down, like an avoidant type, a volatile personality throws it up and out, dumping it onto others.

Irony is also there for volatile types. In all their attempts to control or manipulate others through a strong show of feelings, they most likely generate the results they do not want. Yelling may momentarily control the situation. But there will be a simmering resentment in the other person that ultimately undoes any short-term gains.

Volatility is often about saying and doing things that are destructive in relationships. Things you later regret—that you try to explain you did not really mean. Yet those later apologies seldom undo the damage done.

Sometimes both partners are volatile types. Each is far less bent out of shape when the heat comes on. Yet there are lines that get crossed, and in the blind irrationality of a volatile episode, relationship damage is being incurred.

Avoidance or volatility can occasionally play constructive roles. Especially if it breaks your pattern. If you tend to be impulsively expressive, learning to stand back will represent personal growth and get the respect of your partner. And really speaking up and taking a stand, if that is different for you, may be just the thing to break an impasse.

When you get stuck in a recurrent pattern of one or the other style—you are acting from a very limited inner script. Later in the book, we will discuss moving beyond volatility or avoidance, and give specific tools.

So what happens if one partner is volatile and the other is avoidant? Big problems. Beyond the fundamental downside of each strategy, comes additional suffering due to each person seeing the other's style as wrong.

The person who blows up will push the avoidant one to increasing extremes of avoidance. And the opposite easily happens, with avoidance bringing on escalatingly destructive efforts by the volatile type to break through.

A key for this difficulty is for each type to stop making the other style fundamentally wrong. Realize that both of you have to grow up in some important way.

Staying under cover to avoid rocking the boat is not the same as taking the high ground. Even if avoidance looks good compared to the more obvious destructive consequences of volatility—avoidance has negative consequences.

Making strong, angry statements is also not the better option, compared to what may look like wimping out, staying illusive or being aloof. You may be standing up for your truth, but the delivery you are using—unskilled anger—takes away from your message, and makes it impossible to be heard.

Each of us has to grow. The avoidant needs to stand up more, as the volatile stands down.

• Feeling vs. Thinking
• Emotional vs. Rational
• Emoting vs. Calm

Another very common polarity dance is where one partner operates more from *feeling* and the other from *thinking*.

One partner will tend to be emotional in how they respond to things. They want feelings involved in a relationship, and they pursue knowing what the other feels.

The other person may rely more on logic and rationality. They may be uncomfortable with strong feelings and overt emotionality—not trust it, not want to go there.

This gets played out between two partners in a polarity dance, where one stands on their rational "foot" in opposition to the other's feeling "foot."

In a full-blown polarity dance over feeling vs. thinking, partners end up finding fault with each other. One person may be called "aloof" or "non-feeling"—while the other may be called "irrational" or "hysterical."

The stereotype of gender differences is that women are feeling and men are rational. We found that it can go either way, depending on the personality type of each individual.

The real point, though, is that there is always room for expansion. In a human operating on all cylinders, so to speak, there is feeling and thought, emotionality and rationality.

It is vital for each of us to see if we are internally out of balance, leaning too heavily towards one or the other extreme. A great way to find more balance is to stop fighting the way your partner is and integrate a little more of their style—as uncomfortable as it may be—into your own ways.

- **Emotional Spectrum (anger - hurt - fear)**
- **Specific feelings are OK vs. Not OK**
- **Feelings are Dumped vs. Suppressed**

Many polarity dances are done in the emotional arena. Partners may *specialize* in different feelings, and argue over which feelings are okay versus not okay. One partner may easily display anger, and the other is very uncomfortable feeling it, showing it or even hearing it. The same may be true of the emotion of pain or fear.

I have seen many couples where the following happens. One partner gets hurt but never gets angry. The other partner gets angry but never hurt. Each criticizes the other for having the wrong feelings.

Here it becomes clear that in a polarity dance, people are really fighting over disowned parts of themselves. A whole human has all feelings, but in each of us, some feelings might be consistently suppressed.

According to the gender stereotypes, males and females tend to specialize in different feelings. Boys are trained not to cry and girls not to show anger. When they get together, she may balk at his displaying angry feelings, because she has disowned that emotion in herself. Similarly, he may not be comfortable with her sadness or pain, because he has been cut off from those feelings inside.

When couples do a polarity dance of specialized feelings, one partner ends up feeling the pain for both, while the other carries anger for both. Learning a new dance requires each partner to become more whole, each in touch with their own full human emotional spectrum.

- **Nurturing vs. Authority**
- **Placater vs. Blamer**
- **Mediator vs. Boss**

Placaters want harmony, good feelings, and nurturing. They know what others feel and need. They are mediators. Their body language is hands outstretched, palms exposed, a way of saying, "What do you want or need?"

Blamers look at what people are doing, as far as right or wrong, and tell others how to improve. They are less aware of how others feel. They seem authoritative, bossy or controlling. Their body language is a pointing a finger at the other person, a way of saying, "You are wrong!"

Placaters specialize in hurt feelings, blamers specialize in angry feelings. We have heard name-calling between partners in this dance include "wimp" versus "bulldozer."

When the couple has children, this dance creates conflict over parenting styles. The nurturer is criticized for being too soft—the authoritarian partner for being too hard.

- ## Expression and Solution Styles
- ## Quick vs. Delayed
- ## Pursuer vs. Cave-Dweller

A polarity dance that creates a great deal of unnecessary suffering in relationship has to do with the way in which couples express their feelings and try to solve interpersonal issues. What is being polarized is their timing—and timing is something that is critical to dance. Here, the couple is trying to dance together, but at different speeds.

Their differences in timing makes it difficult for them to solve issues together. One partner needs time to go within and discover what they ultimately feel. They may not be able to get in touch with this inner information in the presence of strong emotions being expressed by the other person. What helps them get to a solution is time, space and quiet. They can tolerate things not being resolved for awhile.

The other partner quickly knows what they feel. They want an immediate solution. They have a low tolerance for things staying in an unsolved state. They may be more emotionally expressive, and put out "loud" emotions.

In the polarity dance around issue solving, one partner pursues the other for immediate answers. That other partner retreats, or gives in to making premature agreements. When the agreement is premature, there can be resentment and a failure to keep it later.

Polarization over timing will make it difficult for couples to reach agreements, make decisions and resolve conflict. Say one partner needs to express all their feelings before they can access the rational part of their brain.

The partner "on the other foot" tries to prematurely reason things out before a logical solution is possible. This partner may even try to convince the more feeling partner that they shouldn't feel the way they do.

Another dance is where the feeling partner wants to know how the more rational partner feels, right now. The rational partner gets accused of not sharing feelings when in actuality they cannot access what they feel on demand.

The above group of polarity dances are all based on unmatched timing around the speed of accessing feelings. One partner is fast, the other slow. Trying to dance at two different speeds, they step on each other's feet.

It's vital to see the underlying factor in these kinds of dances, and then make adjustments to come into better balance with one another over the factor of timing.

• High Energy vs. Low Energy
• Driven vs. Laid Back

Another polarity dance occurs with energetic styles. One partner is very high energy and driven, the other more relaxed and laid back. The differences become the target of value judgments and criticism. One calls the other "lazy." They in turn are called "workaholic" or "obsessive."

Wise partners will recognize how a polarity dance is actually a call for better balance within each individual. But most couples fail to see this and fight it out between one another, as if it were an external battle.

In reality, most of us could probably benefit from a better balance of high and low energy—work and rest—putting out a lot of energy and recharging our batteries.

If we were more willing to see a polarity dance as a call for better internal balance, we could engage in a new form of dance that assisted us each to become more whole.

Perhaps each partner might even be willing to learn from the other those vital new steps that could help them achieve better internal balance and wholeness.

This kind of dancing leads to our personal growth.

• Responsible vs. Spontaneous
• "Uptight" vs. "Irresponsible"

Another polarity dance is being responsible versus being spontaneous. This comes up in decision making. Money conflicts often involve this polarity. One partner suffers the label "uptight"—the other "irresponsible."

The need to plan ahead and feel secure may drive one person, while the other wants to live more in the moment. Frequent disputes result when these two very human sides become split between partners in a polarity dance.

Each partner has only one foot on the ground, each provides only one side of the equation of wholeness. Adding the two of them together looks like one whole, healthy and balanced person—who can be both spontaneous and plan ahead responsibly. The conflict between them is an externalization of each of their internal battles, between a side they are connected with, and a side they are not.

Polarity dances are a result of unclaimed baggage or disowned parts of oneself. A polarity dance between partners is really a sign of the lack of balance within each partner.

- **Perfection vs. Comfort**
- **Orderly vs. Creative**
- **"Rigid" vs. "Sloppy"**

A common polarity dance seems to be between a partner who is more perfectionistic versus one who is more creative or comfort-oriented. This polarization can create conflict over how orderly a home should be kept.

The perfectionist likes order and has a high priority for keeping things cleanly arranged in specific ways. Often they are visually oriented, and like to "keep a tight ship."

Their partner may be a creative cyclone by comparison, with energy for projects but no priority for the visual clean up phase. Another form of this is where partner number two is more into feeling comfortable—being feeling based, not visual in orientation—and finds the overemphasis on order to be stifling.

Name calling frequent accompanies either form of this dance. One partner is called "rigid" and the other "sloppy." Balance may never be found in an ongoing polarity dance around this issue—as long as each party believes their way of doing things is right, and their partner is wrong.

- Extrovert vs. Introvert
- Social vs. Hermit
- Talkative vs. Quiet

This dance tends to occur when a couple differs in social orientation. Some partners seem to be energized by outward connections, perhaps superficial, with numbers of people. They are very comfortable at parties and public events, and enjoy meeting new people.

Other partners are energized by the one-on-one encounter, perhaps in greater depth and with someone they know well. Meeting new people or being at an event where there are many people is not as comfortable to them.

The more introverted partner may also be very comfortable with silence and spending time alone, while the other partner may find both to be uncomfortable.

Extroverted and introverted partners can each learn from each other. Each can come into a more balanced place within themselves, where they could be more comfortable in the full variety of circumstances. But typically they lock into a polarity dance and begin to criticize each other.

• Visual vs. Auditory vs. Kinesthetic

The final set of dances we will look at are a product of the differing strategies by which people mentally represent information. Some people are very visual, externally as well as internally, and may literally think in pictures. They may be very influenced by the exact look of things. Engineers and graphic artists often have a visual orientation.

Other people are more auditory, and pay attention to the sound of things, the exact words that are said, the tone of voice, and may think more in terms of internal dialogue. They may be very influenced by external sound. Musicians are a prime example of this type of person.

A third type of person may be more kinesthetic, paying attention to their gut impressions and sensing how things feel, and their thinking literally is based on the feeling of things. Dancers and athletes tend to be this type of person.

Most relationships are between partners with different orientations. A visual type and a feeling type may polarize into one or more of the dances we have discussed above, never recognizing the simple difference that underlies the majority of their conflicts.

For instance, we saw how the dance of perfection versus comfort may result when a visual type is paired with a feeling type. Each of us can develop our senses and expand the ways in which we represent things.

HOW TO WORK WITH DIFFERENCES

Polarity dances can completely erode your love.

All partners are different, and they have the right to be different. Absolute acceptance of this fact is vital.

Accept the fact of differences. Instead of making the other person wrong, learn to engage in constructive talk about what you need. Later, we will look at how to do this.

A violet and a rose are very different. Yet each is a perfect creation of nature. The violet doesn't need to make the rose wrong, and vice versa—there is nothing to defend.

It may be time to learn a very powerful secret about differences. There's a great potential in having a partner who is different. It gives you the opportunity to expand who you are. It offers you a chance to move beyond your limits—and develop more personal balance and wholeness.

We get a lot of information from the polarity dances we do. Rather than continuing the battle on the outside with a partner, wise partners turn to look within themselves. They take inventory of any wounds, sensitivities and places where they can expand their internal balance.

DECLARE AN END TO WAR

The first step to positive change is to recognize how you are dancing now. Clearly see the part you play, how each step you now take influences where that dance goes.

Professional dancers use mirrors to clearly see how they are dancing. Relationship is like a mirror. If we look clearly into what is going on, we can see our part in it.

Most people have a hard time seeing their own part in a polarity dance. They tend to see the other's role. They may have the belief that to look within is too painful. Or that there's nothing you can do about it anyway.

In relationship, we are more likely to be defensive, rather than being open about our role in things. It seems that if we admitted it, our partner might have something on us, and this may put us at a disadvantage. It seems best to defend or stonewall. This is a great idea for warfare. But how does it help love or nurture our relationship?

At some point, even dedicated soldiers get tired of the

battle and yearn for love. They question warfare and want to find a better way to deal with challenges. An example is the story of how to make soup from stones.

Many years ago three soldiers, hungry and weary of battle, came upon a small village. The villagers, suffering a meager harvest and the many years of war, quickly hid what little they had to eat and met the three at the village square, wringing their hands and bemoaning the lack of food.

The soldiers spoke quietly among themselves and then turned to the village elders. "Your tired fields have left you nothing to share, so we'll share what little we have—the secret of how to make soup from stones."

The villagers were intrigued and soon a fire was put to the town's greatest kettle as the soldiers dropped in three smooth stones. "Now this will be a fine soup," said one soldier, "but a pinch of salt and some parsley would make it wonderful!" Up jumped a villager, crying, "What luck! I've just remembered where some's been left!" And off she ran, returning with an apronful of parsley and a turnip. As the kettle boiled on, the memory of the village improved. Soon barley, carrots, beef and cream had found their way into the great pot, and a cask of wine was rolled into the square as all sat down to feast.

They ate and danced into the night, refreshed by the feast and their new found friends. In the morning the soldiers awoke to find the entire village standing before them. At their feet lay a bag full of the village's best breads and cheese. "You have given us the greatest of gifts, the secret of how to make soup from stones," said an elder, "and we shall never forget." A soldier turned to the crowd and said, "There is no secret: it is only by sharing that we may make a feast."

In polarity dances, we often end up criticizing a partner, being defensive or stonewalling. We act in ways they react to—which escalates the polarization. This is what kills a loving relationship. The results of our own strategies, far from keeping pain away, generate even more pain.

This realization can produce a turning point in some people's lives. They discover that being open and vulnerable is actually empowering. It empowers self-healing, growth, trust, and a deeper sense of connection. And they discover that unexpected rewards flow from owning their part in things— the rewards of greater joy, passion and aliveness.

Take a moment and reflect on the various polarity dances described above. Answer the following questions:

1. **Which upsetting polarity dance seems to be affecting my relationship most at this time?**

2. **Which role do I play in this dance? What are the words and actions associated with my role?**

3. **Which role does my partner play? What are the words and actions associated with their role?**

4. **What result do I get when you increase the intensity of playing my role?**

5. **Am I willing to stretch and grow, to step out of the role I have been playing?**

CHAPTER SIX

REMEMBER THE GOLDEN RULE

"Insanity is doing the same thing in the same way and expecting a different outcome."—CHINESE SAYING

This is only rule you really need to remember:

If what you are doing does NOT result in the loving relationship you truly want...

DO SOMETHING DIFFERENT!

If you keep doing the same old thing, you will keep getting the same old results. You know the road to the Hole and the methods to get there. You also know that every time you do those same things, you end up in that same Hole.

Doing something different is taking a new road. Instead of playing out your normal reaction to an event or situation, do something different. This is the only way you will ever end up in a different place.

It takes courage to do something different, because you won't necessarily know what the right thing is. There may be no one right thing. You can only do this, do that, and see how it works. You cannot know in advance what will work.

You are traveling down an unfamiliar road. Know that it will likely be uncomfortable, at least for awhile. It will require you to expand your resources and skills. It will challenge you to face your fears and stretch your limits.

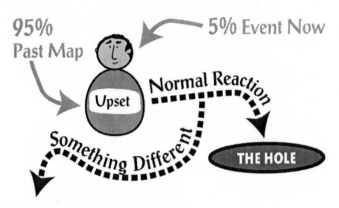

EXPAND YOUR MAP!
- Take a new and different road
- Access your courage
- Move beyond the fear
- Go towards the unfamiliar
- Do this even if there's discomfort

When is the best time to do something different? The signal to do something different is when what you normally do will likely take you to the Hole.

You already know those times. So name them and then stay awake. Figure out what you will do differently when you are in similar situations in the future.

Then do it.

Doing something different is creative and proactive. It is the key that opens the door to the quality of love you want—a passageway out of the Hole and into your dream.

THE JOB DESCRIPTION

1. **NAME WHAT YOU WANT TO CHANGE.** Name the interactions with your partner that take you to the Hole. Review each one—and answer these questions: What does your partner do? What do you do? What do you feel? What do you need? What do they feel? What do they need? Don't guess—ask them what they feel and need.

2. **CLAIM YOUR BAGGAGE.** Discuss these interactions with your partner. Do this when you're outside the Hole and share the intention of claiming baggage to improve things. If you cannot stay out of the Hole with your partner, discuss the problem situations with a friend or counselor. The other person is there to listen. You do most of the talking—and specifically cover the six questions above.

3. **SEE YOUR ROLE.** Get a clear sense of your part in the problem. What specifically do you do in the interaction that adds fuel to the fire? Ask your partner for ideas, or the other person you are discussing things with. Review the section on polarity dances and identify any dance that's a part of your problem interaction. Name your role in that dance.

4. **NAME THE DIFFERENT BEHAVIOR.** Name what you'll do in the future that will be different. Start by asking, "What is the exact *opposite* of what I normally do?" See the following examples for ideas. If you are truly brave and can receive feedback not as demands or criticism, ask your partner for ideas of what might work better.

5. PRACTICE. Don't wait for things to fall apart before you do something different. Under pressure you can forget everything! Be proactive. Set the wheels turning. Find a small circumstance each day that allows you to practice your new behavior. This will help solidify your learning it.

6. STAY AWAKE. Be alert. Don't fall asleep at the wheel. When you find yourself in this type of situation again, see it ahead of time! If you're heading to the Hole, wake up!

7. TAKE THE LEAP. You may get upset just like always. It may be very hard to do anything different. The Hole may be calling you on a molecular level. That's okay. Go ahead and do something different anyway. It's the only way out!

Here are some examples of doing something different:

THE HOLE	SOMETHING DIFFERENT!
Urge to get closer.	Allow some space
Urge to escape	Stay there
Urge to resolve now	Allow some time
Express all feelings	Contain feelings
Hold in feelings	Express feelings
Silent about needs	Voice your needs
Get defensive	Just listen
Try to fix or correct	Just listen
Polarize with partner	Hear their truth

ALLOW SPACE. If you sense your partner is distant and your part of the polarity dance is based on a need to get closer, then something different for you would be to allow space—pull back and be with yourself for awhile.

This is especially important around the feelings of abandonment, a red flag that you are being affected by your baggage. When you feel your partner is not paying you enough attention, you may normally try to close the gap and pursue a connection. This seems to be the way to stop upset feelings of abandonment, but it takes you to the Hole.

Something different is to step back, breathe, center yourself and allow space to be there. Developing this one simple skill will change the relationship. It is your own inner key to transformation!

Remember the way that Jim and Ann transformed their relationship and themselves. They first went to the Baggage Claim Area and told the stories of where their sensitivities for space or distance originated. After naming their patterns, each of them started to learn to do something different.

Jim faced his abandonment issue. Instead of going to the Hole when Ann needed space for her business, he learned to allow that space—and then take care of his own needs. This resulted in deep healing for him. Meanwhile, Ann responded by wanting to find more time to spend together.

STAY THERE. If your part of the dance is based on the need to escape a situation, then something different is to stay there. This is especially true around the feeling of being trapped or wanting to avoid being around emotions, a sign of your 95% factor and old baggage being engaged.

When the situation could potentially bring up certain feelings, you may normally get nervous or just have to leave. You may space out, try to escape in other activities, or even leave the room. You might stonewall or act avoidant in some other way. You may be driven by fear.

Something different is to breathe, center yourself, and simply stay present. There's nothing else you "have to do" while staying there. Just remain present. Developing this one simple ability will change the relationship. It is your personal key to growth.

Ann's part of the pattern with Jim was to want her space for work, but then to need even more space as Jim would get upset about their lack of time together. Her issue was the need to escape a sense of entrapment or control. As she faced her discomfort, she learned to just stay when Jim wanted to share his feelings. In doing so she learned something that was very healing inside herself. Meanwhile, Jim responded with increased ease when she needed space for her business.

ALLOW TIME. If you normally need to resolve a disagreement, upset or conflict immediately, and your partner shows signs of fatigue or needing space, then allow time before a solution is found.

A sure ticket to the Hole is when one person is demanding an answer or resolution before the other is ready. A partner may need time and even space to get in touch with their own truth. To keep going on, pursuing them, will only lead to the Hole.

Something different is to allow them time. Just sit with the situation not being resolved. Step back, breathe and center yourself. Developing this skill will change things.

Remember the story of the boy and the turtle. Pursuing the turtle with a stick was not the way to get it to open. It only went deeper into its shell. But when the boy could just let the turtle have the time to gradually warm up, it popped its head out and started moving.

Allowing time is to face your own sense of urgency for an external resolution. In sitting with the discomfort, and learning to take care of yourself in the meantime, you will discover a powerful healing within. You will also discover that by allowing time, you can reach better solutions.

CONTAIN FEELINGS. If you normally trigger your partner when you express feelings, then practice the art of containing your emotions instead of blurting them out.

Take anger. If you tend to blow up, then contain your anger. This is the old "count to ten" and then some. Leave the situation. Say you need to take a "time out." Then go somewhere else and do something else. Physical activity is good. Don't bring up the subject until you can discuss it with more clarity and calm.

Containment also applies to other emotions, for instance feeling hurt, abandoned or controlled. If you normally go on and on, acting out these feelings with your partner, it's a sign of old baggage and your 95% factor being involved. To your partner, it may feel like you are pushing them into a corner. That leads to the Hole.

Something different is to contain your feelings. Go somewhere else and sit with your feelings. Allow yourself to feel whatever you feel, instead of having to "get it out" by expressing it. As you sit with your feelings, focus on how you can best nurture yourself. Embracing your feelings like this can lead to healing and wholeness within. Developing the skill of containment is a key to changing everything and going down a new road.

Containment is demonstrated in the story of a legendary monk. The students in his monastery were in total awe of this elder monk, not because he was strict, but because nothing ever seemed to upset or ruffle him.

One day they decided to put him to a test. A bunch of them very quietly hid in a dark corner of one of the hallways, and waited for the monk to walk by. Within moments, the old man appeared, carrying a cup of hot tea.

Just as he passed by, the students all rushed out at him screaming as loud as they could. But the monk showed no reaction whatsoever. He peacefully made his way to a small table at the end of the hall, gently placed the cup down, and leaned against the wall.

Then he cried out with shock—"Ohhhhh!"

EXPRESS FEELINGS AND NEEDS. If you normally have a hard time expressing what you feel, something different for you is to verbalize, to share your feelings out loud.

Similarly, if you normally do not express your wants or needs, then something different for you is to verbalize, to ask for what you want or need.

Your partner may sometimes ask you what you feel, and you may tend to avoid trying to talk about it. You might be uncomfortable with emotions in general. Or you may know what you need or feel, but hold it all in. Perhaps you do not want to rock the boat—avoiding potential upsets or conflicts.

Something different for you is to articulate your feelings. Ask for what you want or need. You may stutter and stumble and sound foolish. That's okay. You may risk your partner reacting. That's okay. Developing the skill to verbalize your feelings, wants and needs is your inner key to getting the love you truly want.

Laurie was freshly out of a painful two year relationship. She came to counseling knowing that some of her behaviors had contributed to the pain she experienced. In discussing her past she revealed she was one of eight children and learned very early that her parents were not available for support.

If she was in emotional pain, she withdrew and isolated herself. She learned how to nurture herself, but did not learn how to share her pain with another and receive support. We discussed "do something different"—and her something different was to ask for support when she was in emotional pain, and then be open to receiving it.

She had just begun to date Randy. One evening she was upset and afraid. She decided to take a risk and ask Randy if he could come over and offer support. She made the call and to her surprise, there was silence on the other end. Randy calmly explained that he could not come over, that he had a pattern of rescuing women in distress and he was trying to break that pattern.

Laurie thanked him and hung up the phone. She smiled to herself as she realized that it didn't matter whether Randy came over or not. Her growth and healing was in *asking* for support. She also saw how patterns complement each other and offer an opportunity for both partners to heal.

JUST LISTEN. If you normally try to defend yourself in an interaction, then stop and just listen. Or if you try to fix your partner, trying to make them feel better, then stop and just listen to them.

Often, a trip to the Hole is quickened by one partner trying to change the other. This could be done in the attempt to defend yourself from what they are saying about you. Or it could be inspired by the intention to make them feel better.

Either way, you are interrupting them and attempting to enforce your point of view over theirs. This leads to some kind of right versus wrong scenario, where your partner has to lose or end up feeling unvalidated or unheard.

Your partner may then give up trying to communicate— feeling disconnected. This does little to enhance your mutual love life, and can do long term damage. Or if they have the tenacity, they may keep repeating their message until they think you hear them—which will not happen until you stop trying to convince them they're incorrect.

Something different for you is to just listen. Be quiet and hear whatever they have to say. You don't need to defend or explain yourself. You don't need to take care of their feelings or try to change what they are thinking in any way. Just breathe, center yourself, and listen. Maintain eye contact as much as possible. This skill will be your key to changing everything and finding a new road to travel.

Most people are amazed to discover that doing *less*—just being silent and listening—actually does so much *more* to improve the quality of their love.

The wisdom of listening is not a new idea. In ancient Greece, the philosopher Xenocrates stated, "I have often regretted my speech—but never my silence."

Here's a story to reinforce this point:

A police officer in a small town stopped a motorist who was speeding down Main Street. "But officer," the man began, "I can explain..." "Just be quiet," snapped the officer. "I'm going to let you cool your heels in jail until the chief gets back." "But, officer, I just wanted to say...," "And I said to keep quiet! You're going to jail!"

A few hours later the officer looked in on his prisoner and said, "Lucky for you that the chief's at his daughter's wedding. He'll be in a good mood when he gets back." "Don't count on it," answered the fellow in the cell. "I'm the groom."

HEAR THEIR TRUTH. If you normally polarize with your partner, then something different is to hear their truth. This is a deepening of the skill of just listening. It is where you can actually repeat back to your partner, in their words, what you heard them express.

It's not about translating their message into your words. It's not about outdoing them by saying, "I know exactly what you mean. You think that's something, listen to what happened to me!"

This skill is being able to openly inquire, "Tell me more about that." And saying, "That is really something." This skill will be a key to the transformation of your relationship. It can reveal to you a new road to travel together. There is nothing as validating as to truly be heard. Wise partners know the depth of this human need—and how to meet it.

DEVELOP AN INNER COMPASS

N = New road
Your higher
Intention

S = Same old...
S = Stop!
S = Something different is needed... now!

On the road of relationship, it helps to have a compass. We are talking about an inner tool to tell you if you are headed in a new, positive direction—or to the same old Hole.

Your inner compass tells you whether your behavior in any moment is in true alignment with your higher intention.

How does such a compass signal us?

At first it is easiest to detect if we are headed to the Hole. The signals: negative thoughts, feelings or sensations. You start to see your partner in a negative light. You hear critical voices in your head. It's that knot in your stomach, the pressure in your chest. Or you realize you are holding your breath.

Refine your ability to sense that you are starting to feel upset. It's a feeling something is off in how things are going, the recognition that a familiar pattern is starting up that leads you to the Hole.

There are two marks on your compass: "N" and "S."

They don't refer to North and South.

N stands for "New road"—where you want to travel.

S stands for "Same old..." so "Stop!" and do "Something different... now!"

Beware — be aware — get very conscious whenever you sense you are heading anywhere near the Hole.

If you think you are anywhere near the Hole, pay attention to your compass. Remind yourself of your higher intention (Chapter 2) like "Growth" in this example.

Ask yourself if what you are about to say or do will take you **N** or **S**. Ask if you are truly moving onto a New road, towards your higher intention? Or are you about to do the Same old stuff, moving you further south, to the Hole?

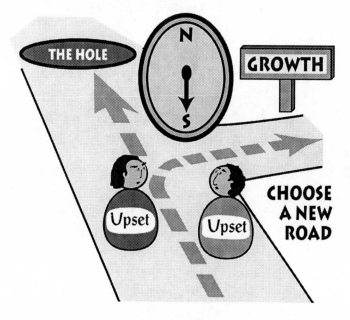

Nobody else can take control of your life—just you.

If you do not want to keep going to the Hole, you need to pay attention to where you are headed.

Don't pretend that your partner is the sole agent of where your relationship is headed. You will only be a victim of circumstances in your mind—not in reality. Because in reality, you are right there, doing what you do in the dance.

So pay attention!

If your compass is pointing to **S**, you need to Stop and do Something different. Try anything different. Do the opposite of what you would normally do. If you are uncomfortable with that, it probably means you are headed in a better direction. It is uncomfortable to do something new and unfamiliar.

DO ANYTHING DIFFERENT

- **Say "Stop!" to yourself and take a Time Out.**
- **Do the opposite of what you normally do.**
- **Ask, "What would I do if I already had achieved personal growth... if I were totally resourceful, healed, free and whole?"**

If nothing seems to work, just say "Stop!" to yourself and take a Time Out. We discuss this in detail later.

A good thing to do is the *opposite* of what you would usually do. What you usually do takes you to the Hole. Try the opposite thing—and see what happens. We saw examples of this in the areas of closeness vs. distance, expressing vs. containing feelings, just listening vs. defending, blaming or fixing, and hearing your partner's truth.

But these are not the only areas of relating where you can benefit by doing something different. Pick any situation that puts you in the Hole. Next, see your part in it. What do you say or do that contributes to the upset? That's where you want to do something different. So what is the opposite of what you usually say or do?

Another way to explore doing something different is to ask yourself, "What would I do if I were totally resourceful, healed and whole?" Imagine how someone else who was centered and confident would behave. Then do that—even though you may not feel centered yourself.

You will be uncomfortable going down a new road. It is unfamiliar. It is different. Feeling uncomfortable is a sign you are going in a new direction.

Remember the story of Sarah and Michael? They were the couple who were driving in the car, where he teased her and then she blew up at him.

Michael's part in the trip to the Hole was to get defensive and think "I'm only trying to lighten things up. Her behavior is totally inappropriate and wrong." Then he blew up back at Sarah. Down the Hole the went.

Something different for him would have been to identify the feeling, "Wow, I see you are angry." Then ask, "What is going on for you right now? Did I say or do anything?"

Next, instead of trying to defend himself, or trying to fix how she felt, or blaming her for being upset—he could have just listened. He could have held his tongue for five minutes, let her speak, and done absolutely nothing else.

Sarah's part in the trip to the Hole was to have a knee-jerk reaction when her 95% factor kicked in from her past. The energy of an old wound suddenly came up, but not realizing this, she thought Michael was the sole source of her upset.

Something different for her would have been to contain

her feelings. Her usual reaction to anger was to immediately and fully express it. If she contained her emotions, she would have been able to process them herself for awhile and then recognize their true source within her.

She might have said, "Your teasing brings up very painful emotions from my past. My father used to abusively tease me as a girl. Anger and hurt from that time is coming back up for me now..."

In telling the whole story, including claiming her past emotional baggage, she might have initiated a trip on the road to Healing rather than the road to the Hole.

Such new behaviors would have brought them closer together and put them on a path of personal growth and positive transformation.

Always keep the Golden Rule in mind...

If what you are doing is not getting you the results you truly want—do something different!

CHAPTER SEVEN

STOP FALLING INTO THE HOLE

"Experience is not what happens to you. It is what you do with what happens to you."—ALDOUS HUXLEY

Many of the ways that we try to communicate do not work. Talking can go in circles for hours, and never get anywhere. The same issue can be discussed over and over—seeming to get resolve, but then coming up again.

How you talk makes a difference.

Partners in great relationships avoid emotional gridlock. They seek out constructive ways to resolve problems and keep the slate clear.

How you communicate is like choosing the road you take. This chapter will give you tools and techniques for how to take a different, more positive road together.

How you act, talk, and express your feelings...

When faced with Challenges and Upset.

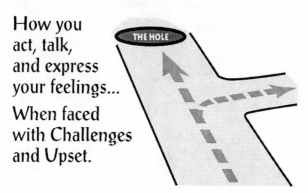

THE HOLE

The road you take is how you act, talk and express your feelings, especially when faced with challenges or upset.

Recall the road that most couples do take when faced with upsets. It's the familiar downward spiral. Partners go around and around the vicious circle until they land in the Hole.

FAMILIAR ROAD
with Challenges and Upset

SAY
Blame
the Other
Person

"Always"
"Never"
"Should"
"Right"
"Wrong"

"You Make
Me Angry!"

DO
Explode
Distance
Pursue
Retreat

SAY
Label
the Other
Person

"You are
Selfish!"

"You are
so Lazy!"

"You are
Insensitive"

THE HOLE

No matter how hard you might try to "work" on things, if you're in the Hole, you can only make matters worse. This is "work" that absolutely *does not work*. The coping strategies you use in the Hole are what *destroy* a relationship.

Specifically, the following behaviors kill love:

• Blame the other person

You blame your partner for causing the situation. Like, "You make me angry!" or "You ruined our entire vacation!" or "You frustrate me!"

• Label or Criticize the other person

You put a negative label on your partner, like "insensitive" or "selfish" or some other critical name-calling. Like, "You are uptight!" or "You're such a slob!"

• Be defensive, Win-Lose, "right" vs. "wrong"

You try to defend yourself or prove your partner is wrong. Like, "That's your problem!" or "What about when you did such and such" or "You're wrong!" or "You never do it right."

• Stonewall, shut down & distance

You shut down, walk out, avoid the issue, pretend it's not important, minimize, or simply fail to listen and understand what your partner is saying.

• Generalize, Black-and-White

You have moved beyond talking about the specific event and are making generalized statements. There are some classic red-flag words—"always," "never," "should," "right" and "wrong"—words that reveal you have collapsed into black and white thinking. Statements get dramatized or overgeneralized. You say things like, "You *never* help me around here!" "I'm *always* cleaning up after you!"

Research has shown that continued use of these coping strategies leads to divorce or separation. In other words, if you want to split up, communicate like this.

You have previously read about this road in depth, all the way down to the bottom of the Hole. Faced with challenges or upsets, partners become reactive. Their 95% factor kicks in from the past and amplifies emotions to a level where it is impossible to interact in a constructive way.

Instead of getting to a positive resolution, partners dig themselves in deeper. They blame and criticize one another, each seeing the other person as the cause of the upset. They get defensive, distance or stonewall.

Couples in the Hole are dominated by their reactivity. The "fight or flight" reaction alters body-brain chemistry. It alters how we talk and act. We are *under the influence*—chemicals have taken over and deleted our rational capacity.

In other words, you are simply trying to cope with the anxiety in your body—and you are no longer capable of any form of communication that will get a positive result.

In the Hole, there is no possibility of a mutual solution. Each person wants to be "right" and therefore the other must be proven "wrong." Someone has to "lose" and nobody feels accepted. It is clear from the outside that partners are only damaging their love.

In the Hole, our positive options are sharply reduced—if not gone altogether. Yet, people keep trying to resolve the situation, as if they could! Each wants to put in the final word. Emotions escalate. Someone may explode or leave.

Most of us can recognize one or more of these strategies. They seem like normal things to do when you are upset. But be warned. They can damage love beyond repair.

Unless you develop different strategies to resolve issues, the strategies of the Hole will either destroy your partnership, or leave you sharing long term unhappiness.

In my practice, when I first see couples I often hear reports from the Hole. I ask if they know Rule One for what to do if you are stuck in a deep hole. They usually look at me with blank expressions on their faces....

Rule One is this: "Stop Digging!"

FIRST STEP TO A DIFFERENT ROAD
with Challenges and Upset

The first step to a different road when facing challenges and upsets is to recognize the damaging effect of reactivity and the 95% factor. See the Hole, don't pretend it's not there, and don't let yourself be tempted to jump into it!

Trying to solve anything in the Hole is like trying to balance spinning plates when you are fall-over drunk. Emotional reactions alter the chemistry of the body and mind just as surely as any strong intoxicant.

Talking from the Hole, partners end up saying things they later regret and perhaps didn't even mean. The damage from the discussion about the problem can be far worse than the problem itself. Partners misunderstand one another more often than not, and further inflame the issue.

The attempt to solve things once reactivity has kicked in is like trying to put a fire out by throwing gasoline on it. It is vital for partners to recognize and admit they do more damage than good when they go down the road to the Hole. Then agree to do something different!

RULE ONE: STOP DIGGING!

I often ask couples, "Can you remember one time when you went into the Hole and resolved an issue in a mutually satisfactory way?"

Usually there is silence...

Then I ask, "Can you name times when you went into the Hole and things just continued to get worse?" There is no shortage of reports where upsets escalated beyond control. Things said were taken the wrong way and there didn't seem to be any way to get through and be understood. Partners were left in an emotionally exhausted state, with even more to deal with than the original problem.

When we go into the Hole, we are being dominated by issues and emotions from the past. What we are trying to resolve has less to do with a current partner than it does with deep seated old wounds. We are most likely trying to resolve old wounds with parents or others from our past.

Yet the way we project that onto our partner now will only hurt our current love. Are you convinced yet that there is absolutely nothing that will be solved inside the Hole? Do you want to travel on a different road? If so, read on...

THE "TIME OUT" TOOL

To travel on a new road, you must stop moving toward the Hole. This is the very first step. You need to take this step before you can begin to go in a new direction.

Let's say you find, unexpectedly, that you are involved in a situation where one or both of you are getting upset. You may already be going around the Vicious Circle. Or you may be at the starting line, about to engage in a familiar trip to the Hole.

Someone has just said or done something, and the other person is getting upset. The Time Out tool is what will keep you out of the Hole.

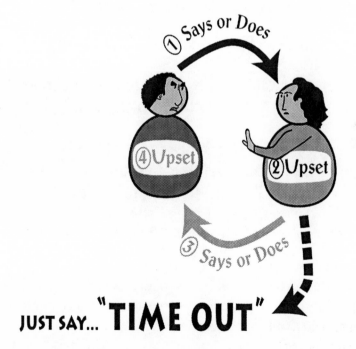

JUST SAY... **"TIME OUT"**

What you do is just say "Time Out" That's it.

If this sounds too simple, you are right.

It is just that simple.

It is an unusual thing to do, and therefore it will not be as comfortable as continuing to head into the Hole. Incredibly, couples are more comfortable with the familiar escalation to crisis, than with an unusual act like saying "Time Out"

You and your partner need to set up a Time Out agreement for this tool to be effective. We discuss that below. You will also have to learn to say and hear the words "Time Out" in ways that avoid further triggering emotional reactions.

But the hardest thing will be to remember to do it.

Let's address the actual meaning of saying "Time Out"

INTENTION OF SAYING "TIME OUT"

"Time Out" = "I'm not resourceful enough right now to hear you..."

- **Recognize you're headed for the Hole**
- **Ask for time out to get centered**
- **Say you'll return to the topic later**
- **You want to reach a positive result**
- **You want to honor your higher intention**

Saying "Time Out" is the same as saying:

"I'm not resourceful enough right now to hear you. I'd like to return to this topic later. If we continue discussing it now, I am afraid I will only end up in the Hole."

"I would like some time out now so I can center myself."

"Then I would like to return to this topic in a few hours—when I will be able to better hear and understand what you are saying—and respond in a resourceful way."

"I want to reach a positive result with you around this topic—one that works for both of us."

"Is it okay with you if we continue discussing this in three hours? Or is there a better time for you?"

Depending on your level of upset and anxiety, you may need more time before getting back to discuss the topic. Maybe you'll need to take a break—be alone and center yourself. At other times, you may only need to change the topic of conversation or be silent for a few minutes.

The important thing is to *stop* moving toward the Hole.

Saying "Time Out" is like putting a stop sign in front of the Hole. It says, "Wake up! We are about to go into the Hole if we keep going in the same direction."

Later on, when you are well practiced in the Time Out tool, you can learn to put up a detour sign or fluidly move around the Hole. You can even learn to take an abrupt right turn and travel down a new road.

The Time Out tool is the first step.

When I had recurrent back pain, my physical therapist told me, "If you want to start healing your back, you need to stop doing more damage to it. Stop lifting heavy objects!"

It seems pretty obvious now. And it worked. So does the Time Out tool. If you want to start truly resolving issues, you need to stop adding more damage to your love. Trying to resolve issues when you're in the Hole is the equivalent of lifting heavy objects when your back is already out.

MAKE A TIME OUT AGREEMENT

To use the Time Out tool effectively, a couple needs to make a clear, specific agreement. This means writing up the agreement as a contract and signing it.

What should be included in such a contract appears on the next page. The contract begins by stating its purpose—to stop engaging in behaviors that destroy your relationship and to act in a way that honors your own higher intentions (Chapter 2), as well as your shared vision (Chapter 11).

The contract goes on to declare the specific behavioral agreements that support its purpose. These are all necessary for the Time Out tool to actually work.

Partnership Agreement

Purpose:
To Stop Destructive Behavior
To Honor Your Shared Vision

Terms:
- Pick a Signal ("Time Out").
- It is Absolute. You Must Stop.
- Your job to say "Time Out" ASAP... as soon as you feel yourself react.
- Whoever says "Time Out" proposes a time to come back together.
- Time Out = 1 hour - 24 hours.
- You must come back as agreed.

There are six ingredients required to make a complete Time Out agreement. If you leave one of these out—or fail to observe it—the Time Out tool will not work.

1. Pick a verbal signal. This can be the words "Time Out" or anything else ("Please Stop", "Whoa!") if you come up with other words that work better for you. It should be short and clearly identifiable in any context.

2. You agree that when this verbal signal is given by either person, you *both* will immediately stop no matter what is happening. There needs to be no further explanation of why one of you has called "Time Out." No justification is required. You already understand the full meaning of the verbal signal and the intention behind using it. There is no debate. It is absolute. You stop discussing the topic immediately!

3. It is your job to say "Time Out" as soon as possible— whenever you sense things are moving in the direction of the Hole. You must say it as soon as you realize *you* are starting to react. You don't wait or think, "We can solve this if I can just make my point" or "I can take a little more of this..." You say "Time Out" Hesitation to do this is the main failing point of most couples in using the Time Out tool. We will talk more about this below.

4. Whoever calls "Time Out" proposes the time and place to come back together in order to address the issue in a more resourceful way. It is then their primary duty to get centered in order to better hear the other partner.

5. Ideally, the time out period should be at least one hour, but not more than 24 hours. You can agree to exceptions. Work within the schedules of each partner to find a time where you both are most likely to be resourceful.

If you use third party counseling or coaching, it may be better to take the issue to session. You might more easily resolve the issue and learn new communication skills at the same time.

In the beginning, some couples we work with declare several "Time Out's" during the week and postpone resolution until they see us. They report that they continue to interact in loving ways in the meantime, feeling like a weight has been lifted off their backs.

6. You must come back as agreed. The Time Out tool is not a method for avoiding important issues. It's a way to stay resourceful and on the 5% level of feelings where you can still successfully negotiate wants and needs and find mutual resolution. It's a way to keep the heat of the 95% factor from kicking in, amplifying your emotional states and taking you into the Hole.

USE IT OR LOSE IT

Partners often hesitate or forget to say "Time Out" This is the main failing point I have seen. You've got to use it or you will lose it. By "losing it" we mean you'll fall in the Hole.

The story of the four monks shows how easily we can be sidetracked from keeping an agreement to take time out. The four agreed to meditate silently without speaking for two weeks. By nightfall on the first day, the candle began to flicker and then went out. The first monk said, "Oh, no! The candle is out." The second monk said, "Aren't we not suppose to talk?" The third monk said, "Why must you two break the silence?" The fourth monk laughed and said, "Ha! I'm the only one who didn't speak."

For it to work, you have to remember to keep the Time Out agreement. Some people may think saying "Time Out" is an act of copping out or showing weakness. Others may be afraid they could insult their partner or further rock the boat. So they just "forget" to say it.

But saying "Time Out" is a gift to the relationship, and to each other. It stops an all too predictable journey to the Hole before more harm is done. It sets up an interval of time for you to get perspective and center yourselves, so that you can later address the issue and get a more positive result.

So, to repeat, it is your job to say "Time Out" as soon as you sense things are headed to the Hole. If you are operating on a 5% level of emotions, appropriate to what is going on here and now, you can still achieve a positive result. As soon as you hit 10% and rising, you are closing in on the Hole.

You may start to feel sensations in your body that tell you the discussion is more heated than the issue warrants. A tightness in your throat or stomach, perhaps. Say "Time Out" If you wait until you hit 25% or 50%, it's already too late. It takes only 10 seconds for the 95% factor to fully kick in. By then you are lost!

Say conflict arises over not keeping the house as clean as the other wants. Maybe it's about that pair of socks discovered on the living room floor. At 5%, you can negotiate and find a mutual solution. At 10%, you may start hearing the words "You always..." or "You never..."

Remember Rule One. It's time to say "Time Out"

If you hesitate, hoping things will be different this time, you are just fooling yourself. You are pretending the Hole is not there. Say "Time Out"—Stop Digging!

It is your job to say "Time Out" Remind each other to take time out and return to the topic later when you can be more centered. You both can do things differently and create for yourselves a better chance to get a positive result.

PRACTICE MAKES PERFECT

When nurses initially learn to do CPR, cardiopulmonary resuscitation, they practice doing it over and over again—on a dummy. This allows them to integrate the new behavior so that they can perform it later in the heat of emergency.

It would make no sense to start learning CPR directly on a patient in critical condition. Similarly, it makes no sense to try to integrate the Time Out tool into your behavior by waiting until things heat up before you use it.

I recommend practicing a mock Time Out—once a day for a month. This is where you say "Time Out" but you are not feeling upset. You are just practicing the tool, so that you can more easily do it later, under fire.

It's great if you can practice a mock Time Out at a time when it seems to fit a situation, before there is any emotional upset. But this really doesn't matter. Whether or not such perfect situations arise, it is important to practice it every day.

Since this is a *mutual* agreement, your partner will also be practicing, and this will help you adjust to hearing the word "Time Out" and then respecting it rather than getting upset.

In a mock Time Out, simply say your signal—"Time Out" or whatever you have chosen. Then follow it up with, "I need to take some time out here, to get more resourceful. Can we continue this topic in five minutes?" Then leave the room if possible, or at least be completely silent for a full five minutes. During that time, breathe and center yourself.

CONSIDER THE ALTERNATIVE

Many people tell us "I called a Time Out, but I still felt very upset. So what's the point of saying Time Out? It didn't get rid of my upset feelings."

We have one answer. Consider the alternative.

If you went further into the Hole, do you seriously think you would end up feeling less upset? Be honest. You are only going to get more and more upset—as you and your partner say more and more unresourceful things to each other.

The sooner you stop your march to the Hole, the less upset you will have, the less time it will take you to get resourceful, and the less damage you will have to try to undo.

Why don't we all realize this?

Because the Hole is very seductive and tricky.

The Hole says "Jump in here! This is the way to get rid of your upset feelings. Act them out! Blame your partner!"

But the Hole is lying to you. Has that ever been true? Even once, have you resolved something from inside the Hole?

So, sure, you will say "Time Out" and then you'll still have whatever upset you are feeling in the moment. In the silence of a Time Out, you may even be more aware of them.

But consider the alternative—creating even more upset feelings and more damage. And creating even more loss of love and self-esteem.

Don't let the Hole trick you into thinking you can get rid of your upset if only you prove you are right, or yell loud enough, or dump your judgments onto your partner.

Consider the alternative to Time Out—increasing damage.

Then do the wise thing and say "Time Out"

ALL TIME OUTS ARE SELF-STOPS

The real secret to the Time Out tool is that you are actually stopping yourself. It is vital to see the true inner reason that you personally have for using the Time Out tool.

That reason is simply this:

You don't want to go to the Hole!

If you have read this far, you realize that going to the Hole is destructive to your relationships. But that's only half the story. The rest is just about you.

Going to the Hole is destructive to your mental well-being and probably even your physical health. Each step you take towards the Hole sets you up for more inner suffering, more mental rumination, more replays of your inner movies, more tension in your body, more stress on your heart.

Going to the Hole makes you act and talk in ways you will personally regret. Each step you take towards the Hole lowers your personal self-esteem and stunts your personal growth.

Here is the bottom line. Going to the Hole means you have just forgotten your own true higher intention!

How are you taking a new road of "Growth" or "Healing" if you are letting yourself go to the Hole again? No matter what your higher intention (Chapter 2) is, you are not going to find it in the Hole. There, you will only find yourself in a less resourceful, contracted condition.

Is that how you want to live your life? Unconscious? Out of alignment with who you truly want to be?

When you stop yourself from taking just one more step

towards the Hole, you make a conscious choice that supports your own personal growth and your higher intention.

So anytime you say use this technique, you are really saying "Time Out" to yourself—for yourself. Saying this is a way of taking good care of yourself.

Whether or not your partner is ready to join you in a Time Out, you still owe it to yourself to stop. Sometimes this may mean being silent unilaterally, or even leaving the room.

If you have to take a unilateral time out, don't just walk away or slam the door. Clearly state you are taking a time out to go center yourself. Announce that once you calm down, you will come back to listen to your partner.

Ultimately, you are a part of how the interaction is going, and you are responsible to take care of yourself.

IN THE HEAT OF EMOTION

Aristotle said, "Anybody can get angry, that is easy. But to be angry to the right degree, and at the right time, and for the right purpose, and in the right way—that is not within everybody's power and is not easy."

Communicating anger is especially problematic for many relationships. One partner may be sensitive to anger and may get quite hurt by it. Unless both partners really enjoy yelling, the way anger gets expressed will be an important factor that can determine whether love builds—or decays.

Avoiding conflict is certainly not the solution. Research indicates that couples who avoid conflict are prone to divorce. Avoidance results in distancing further and further, until love seems lost. Studies also show that couples who stay married have as many conflicts as those who divorce. The difference is the skill level they bring to communicating.

Anger is a natural emotion and needs to be expressed—in a skillful way. Anger is an important signal that something is not working for us, that we are not getting our needs met, or that our boundaries are being crossed.

Sharing these signals with one another is as vital as using indicator lights when driving a car. Letting each other know what is going on, gives the other a chance to respond.

It is not the emotion of anger itself that damages love. The real issue is *how* it gets expressed, the specific actions and words that accompany the anger.

There is a story about a little boy with a bad temper. His father gave him a bag of nails and told him that every time he lost his temper, to hammer a nail in the back fence. The first day the boy drove 37 nails into the fence.

Then it gradually dwindled down. He found it was easier to hold his temper than drive those nails into the fence. Finally the day came when the boy didn't lose his temper at all. He told his father, who suggested the boy now pull out one nail for each day that he was able to hold his temper.

Days passed and the young boy was finally able to tell his father that all the nails were gone. The father took his son by the hand and led him to the fence.

He said, "You have done well, my son, but look at the holes in the fence. The fence will never be the same. When you say things in anger, they leave scars like these. You can put a knife in a man and draw it out. It won't matter how many times you say 'I am sorry'—the wound is still there."

The Time Out tool helps develop a level of skill in the

expression of anger. It helps you to pull back from the brink of the Hole, to stop yourself from acting out the anger on automatic pilot.

When you take time out, it is your job to get centered and resourceful, so you can come back together and express your message with skill. After all, if it was important enough to blow up about, it's important enough to express well.

There are countless recommendations for how to work through anger during a time out—from writing about it to engaging in physical exercise or activity of some sort. Go for a brisk walk. Chop firewood. Do something productive that you have been putting off.

Some people benefit by just sitting for awhile, breathing, and feeling all the sensations in their belly. Find out and do whatever works for you. The next chapter gives you a powerful method to center and calm yourself.

If you are in relationship with a partner who is willing to make a Time Out agreement, write the following on a sheet of paper, date it, sign it and put it somewhere special:

YOUR TIME OUT AGREEMENT

1. The signal will be _____ (e.g. "Time Out").
2. It will be absolute. I will stop if you give the signal.
3. I will give the signal as soon as I feel I am in the reaction zone and am going to the Hole.
4. Whoever gives signal proposes when to come back together to discuss topic more resourcefully.
5. Time out period is between one hour and 24 hours.
6. I will come back as agreed.

CHAPTER EIGHT

CENTER YOURSELF

*"Are you willing to feel better—
even if everything outside of you stays the same?"*

All relationships run into problems or differences. These often give rise to upset feelings. We may feel angry, frustrated, irritated, hurt, sad, resentful, afraid, ashamed, condemning, or a range of other negative feelings.

If these feelings are strong, the chances are very good that past sensitivities or wounds have become activated and are adding into our emotional mix. Such unhealed issues from our past amplify our negative feelings to new heights.

How each individual faces and handles their negative feelings will determine how a relationship fares over time. The way in which we deal with our upsets is a key element in the longterm success—or failure—of a relationship.

Unfortunately, many of us have poor training to deal with negative feelings. This chapter presents a tool which you can use to center yourself, soothe your anxieties, calm yourself down—and find your inner resourcefulness.

OUTER AND INNER TOOLS

Most relationship skills currently taught have to do with improving communication. Communication is an event that occurs between two people. It is usually seen as the main issue when things get upsetting in a relationship.

However, poor communication arises from the upset emotions each partner is feeling within themselves.

It is our inner world—our upset emotional state—that drives bad communication. When we fall into the Hole, we are interacting from a place of "fight or flight." The resulting body chemistry takes control over our words and actions.

In this condition, the good communication techniques you know are out of reach. Communication skills are "outside" tools, used to be effective in the external world.

What you need when upset are vital "inside" tools.

If a relationship is plagued with negativity, the driving force pushing it downhill is unresolved emotional upset. If this upset is not transformed or shifted, communication skills alone will fail to turn things around.

Upset emotions live within us. They are best transformed using "inside" tools.

THE SOLUTION IS WITHIN YOU

When upset, we usually focus on what needs to change outside of ourselves. We want the other person or the situation to change—so we can feel better inside.

This "outside" approach typically fails. So our negative feelings continue to build. After an upsetting event we rehash things in our mind or rehearse what to say or do next. This keeps us upset, even makes us more upset.

If our attention is placed on the outer event and the other person, this keeps us from transforming our own inner world. We may not realize there's a way to directly work with, soothe, heal and shift our inner feelings.

Feelings live within us. To transform them we must first place our attention within our inner world.

Below, you will learn a new and powerful "inside" tool to help you calm and soothe your internal feelings. This tool has been known and used for thousands of years—and is being rediscovered by psychologists today.

Ultimately, it's your world—there within you. Why not learn all you can to take the best possible care of it?

When upset, you may want changes to happen outside yourself, from your partner. Such changes indeed may be desirable. Regardless, consider the following statement:

Relationship is an "Inside Job"

This means we will never succeed in longterm love if we do not master our own inner feelings—and learn to soothe, heal and calm what comes up inside of us.

When we finally wake up to the possibility of taking inner care of our emotional upsets—then we can make changes that will profoundly affect our outside world of relationships. When we give up blaming others, and trying to change who they are so we can feel better, the outside world of relationships can shift in a positive direction.

This is a paradox. To change a relationship, the change starts within you. Love starts within yourself.

We are not suggesting that you should allow people to behave in a way that does not work for you. On the contrary, you are responsible to assert healthy personal boundaries, and to constructively communicate what works for you.

In making the statement that relationship is an "inside job" we encourage you to learn to work with your upset feelings. When you do this, you end destructive emotional entanglement and show up in a healthy, powerful way. That feels good! And it changes everything on the outside for the better.

AN INNER TOOL

Here is a simple, powerful tool: the In & Down process.

This is a tool you can use under any circumstances, to center yourself and calm your inner world. It helps you hold onto yourself and not get lost in negative feelings.

In & Down is a process you can use anywhere, anytime you start to feel yourself emotionally react. It gives you a way to contact and build your inner strength.

It involves training your attention to move at will, so you do not lose yourself in emotional upset. With practice, you can develop mastery to stay centered within a resourceful state—instead of getting lost or acting out in ways you later regret.

A tool like In & Down is used by Tai Chi masters, Akido black belts, Buddhist monks, and many other traditions of self-mastery. Today, this inner tool is used as a method for stress reduction and for self-calming. Helen Palmer, a leading authority on the Enneagram personality system, teaches this tool as a method to move beyond habitual personality patterns which trap us in upset and suffering.

WE LEARNED HOW TO GET UPSET

The ways we emotionally react, suffer and get upset are not preordained. They are not set in stone. They are learned in childhood. As adults, we can now learn new ways to respond.

Between two and eight years old, we learn what "should"

upset us and how we should react—with anger, jealousy, insecurity, avoiding conflict, withdrawing from emotions, getting hysterical, feeling trapped, fearing abandonment, resentment, and all the other reactions we suffer.

Many of the problems in adult relationships directly reflect this childhood training. It is literally as if we are still driven by an "inner six year old" when it comes to love.

Most of this upset and suffering is unnecessary.

And there is good news. Since the ways we tend to react and suffer were learned in childhood—this means that we can now learn healthier ways to respond.

If you are committed to changing yourself from the inside, you can learn to vastly reduce your tendencies to get upset or react the way you usually do. With practice over time, you can achieve powerful, positive results.

Consider committing to take charge of your inner life, to learn the right tools—and to use them.

CHOOSE TO CENTER YOURSELF

The In & Down process is a powerful inner tool to center yourself if you begin to get upset. It can help you self-soothe and calm yourself down. Using In & Down, you can find a peaceful place in a potential emotional storm.

Think of types of "emotional storms." Some are active, like thunder and lightning—with bolts of anger or tidal waves of anxiety or pain. Others seem more foggy or frozen—where we find ourselves numbing out, withdrawing, stuck in upset feelings or incapacitated with confusion.

An emotional storm is like rolling waves on the ocean—

rocking and tossing you in their wake. Instead of getting lost in the waves—the In & Down process is like going down into the depths of the sea to a resting place on the calm sandy ocean floor, where all is still, regardless of stormy waves above. We will return to the ocean metaphor again, later.

In essence, it is knowing how to hold onto who you truly are, regardless of the stress of your circumstances or how poorly others may be acting. It is taking responsibility for your own inner mental and emotional health—in each moment.

WARMUP EXERCISE

Here is a warmup experience that will prepare you to learn In & Down. It only takes five minutes. We assume you are in a room right now. If not, do your best to apply the following.

After you read each sentence, stop and close your eyes and move your attention to where it says—and hold your attention there for about five seconds before opening your eyes and continuing to the next sentence:

1. **Place your attention in the center of the room.**

2. **Place your attention against the far wall.**

3. **Place your attention at book-reading distance.**

4. **Put your attention on your feet and try to find out which foot feels lighter—your right or your left.**

There is no "right" answer or anything you "should" feel.

Now review these four placements of attention. If possible keep your eyes closed. Notice any differences as you put your attention: (1) in the center of the room; (2) on the distant wall; (3) at book-reading distance; (4) on your feet.

The next step is to explore more "inside" placements of your attention. Three will be on thoughts in your head, and one will be on your breathing.

As before, read each of the following sentences. Then close your eyes and put your attention on where it says—and keep it there for about five seconds:

1. **Put your attention on a thought or memory of an event from this past week.**

2. **Put your attention on a thought about the future, on something you are planning to do next week.**

3. **Put your attention on a thought that is entirely imagined, on something that you make up.**

4. **Put attention on your breathing. Notice where in your body you feel yourself inhale and exhale.**

As before, there is nothing you "should" feel. If you had trouble locating your breath, try to sense either how fast or slow it is, and whether it is deep or shallow.

Now review these four placements of attention. Again, do this with your eyes closed. Put your attention on: (1) a memory of a past event; (2) a future event; (3) something you imagine; (4) on your breath.

How was it different in any way between thinking of the past, the future, something imaginary? How was it different from these to attempt to put your attention on your breath?

The final warmup experience is entirely about different locations of your breath. As before, read each of the following sentences, then close your eyes and put your attention on what it instructs and keep it there for about five seconds:

1. **Put your attention on your chest and how it expands and contracts with each breath. Notice the speed of breathing and the depth of each breath.**

2. **Put your attention lower, somewhere between your chest and your belly and sense any movement with each breath. Notice the speed and depth.**

3. **Move your attention to your belly and sense even the slightest movement there with each breath. Notice the speed and depth of your breathing there.**

4. **Let your attention rest on the floor of your belly, about an inch or two below your belly button. Sense any movement there with each breath.**

Now review these four placements of attention, with your eyes closed. This time as you do it, let your attention linger in each location for a longer time. Put your attention on your breath: (1) in your chest; (2) midway to your belly; (3) in your belly; (4) at the bottom floor of your belly, slightly below the naval. Let it stay there for a minute.

DIRECT YOUR ATTENTION

In the experience, first you put your attention "outside" in the room. Then you moved "inside" to your thoughts. Finally, you moved to your body and sensed your breathing, moving down until you got to the floor of your belly.

Resting there, you can get more centered and clear, calm and resourceful. Acting from this inner placement of attention, you can achieve better results on the outside.

The section on the next page—"In & Down"—will take you through the process step by step. Do not worry about "getting it right" because however you do it is okay. It will feel more and more powerful the more you practice it.

If you have a voice recorder, record the following page at a slow pace. Then play it back to yourself to be guided through the process. Just close your eyes and get into it.

If you are in a relationship, I recommend reading this for each other. Or if you have a friend who will read it to you, that is another good way to get it.

Otherwise, just read to yourself, and go at your own pace. Get your own sense of how the process works by doing each step as you read it. Just pause and close your eyes as you experience each step fully.

Sit comfortably in a chair, and place your feet flat on the floor. Go through this slowly.

The full process is on the next page. The final step in it suggests you keep your eyes closed as you continue doing the process for a few additional minutes. By then you can just close your eyes and fully enjoy the process until it seems time to reopen your eyes.

IN & DOWN PROCESS

Notice where your attention is placed. On a sound? On a thought? On a feeling? On a sensation? Just notice this.

Bring your attention in and down, to your chest. Notice your breathing there. Is it deep or shallow? Fast or slow?

Move your attention down into your belly. Notice your breathing there. Sense the slight rise or fall of your belly as you breathe in and out.

Now move your attention to the floor of your belly—to an inch below your naval. Sense how the floor of your belly slightly rises and falls with each breath. Your task now is to your attention here, at the bottom of your belly.

If you realize your attention has wandered to a thought, just say "that's a thought." Then choose not to follow it. Just gently move your attention back in and down, to the floor of your belly. Notice your breath there.

Over the next few minutes, whenever you notice you have been hooked by a thought, just say "that's a thought." Then move back in and down, and pay attention to the floor of your belly. Notice its slight rise and fall with each breath. Keep your attention in and down for a few minutes more. Sense this deeper by closing your eyes. After a few minutes, open them again, while keeping your attention focused in and down.

THE SANDY OCEAN FLOOR

The practice of In & Down helps you become more centered and solid within yourself.

There are numerous metaphors to describe the process of going In & Down. Consider an ocean and its waves. When we are not centered, we may feel like we are a ping-pong ball being tossed about on the waves of an ocean.

Waves of thoughts hook us and lead us into upset states. Waves of emotion may grab us. Getting caught up in thoughts and feelings, we will lose all semblance of inner peace and emotional resourcefulness.

There is an alternative. Go In & Down.

To go In & Down is like diving into the ocean, going all the way down to the bottom, and landing on the sandy ocean floor. At the bottom of the ocean there is calm and stillness.

No matter how choppy the waves above, no matter how stormy the weather conditions, when you dive down to the bottom of the ocean, and sink your feet into its sandy floor— you come to rest in stillness.

Going In & Down is to choose to unhook your attention from the traps of thoughts or feelings, to move out of your head and into your body. You go all the way down to the center of who you truly are, and come to rest there.

As you remain resting at your center, a natural sense of spaciousness gradually unfolds. You may start to feel more connected to the chair you are sitting in, or the floor you are standing on.

Each successive breath feels more and more free. You relax into the moment and discover peace.

FOCUS ON YOUR BREATH

Each time our attention gets hooked by a thought, we are either taken into the past or future. This increases anxiety and upset. We worry about what might happen. We fume over what already happened.

What positive results do we ever get doing this? The future is unknown. The past is over and cannot be changed.

When you move your attention back to the breath, there is only the one breath you are breathing—right here, right now. A past or future breath is no consequence.

When you come fully into this breath right now, you arrive in the present moment. You expand to be more fully present within your actual living experience, here and now.

If you pay close attention right now, you may discover you are actually okay—regardless of what is going on outside. So whenever thoughts or feelings hook you, move your attention back In & Down. Put it on your breath.

Think of the cycle of breathing. Imagine it takes the form of a wave, as it moves from exhale to inhale and back again. There is a peak and a valley of that wave. This corresponds to how the floor of your belly rises and falls in each breath.

When you go In & Down, discover exactly where in the cycle of the breath you feel the most space, stillness and calm. At the peak? At the valley? Somewhere in between?

Discover where the exact point of maximum stillness is. It may vary from time to time. Wherever it is, put your focus on that part of the breathing cycel. Put more of your attention on it, and gently let yourself embrace the full spaciousness, calm and stillness it is offering you.

PRACTICE MAKES SKILLFUL

You should now have a sense of In & Down. Hopefully you got to feel a bit more centered and calm. Don't worry if this does not happen yet. Accept however it goes.

Practice In & Down several times a day. One time could be where you sit down and do it for five minutes, as a meditation. The point is to use it in your daily life—not just to make some kind of separate, speical meditation practice out of it.

Find times in daily life where it can help you.

Do you get frustrated waiting in line? Use the In & Down process. You could be delighted with increased feelings of peace and joy.

How about using it in traffic jams? After you learn to do In & Down, you won't have to close your eyes to do it.

What about meetings that you don't enjoy? In & Down can change your negative feelings to more resourceful feelings. Chances are, you'll get more effective results, too.

There are lots of places to practice In & Down as a tool in daily living. The more busy you are, the more you can benefit from it. In & Down will increase your ability to be centered, resourceful and feel good. When is that not useful?

Like all skills, you get better at In & Down the more you practice. So practice it every day.

When we are upset, our normal placement of attention is outside ourselves, and may be on the past or future. We focus on how the other person or the situation needs to change. We fume over the past. We fret about and try to plan the future.

This doesn't actually help. Quite the contrary. But once mastered, In & Down can help.

For most of us, it seems perfectly reasonable to have an external focus if there's a problem. We think, "Get the other person to change. They are the reason we're upset."

How well does this work? Terribly. It usually leads to more upset and suffering. And negative results.

Moving attention In & Down is a much better strategy.

In & Down is powerful when you are in the middle of a hard situation. It's also useful if you are replaying an event in your head. If you find yourself getting upset in such reviews, you'll do better by moving your attention In & Down.

This tool helps you get centered and shift upset feelings. That's a big payoff in life. So practice!

TIME OUT FOR IN & DOWN

Say a difficult interaction moves you towards the Hole, and you call for a "Time Out."

You will likely still have upset feelings.

Use In & Down during the time out period. This helps you calm down and soothe yourself. It helps you really figure out what is important to communicate. It helps you regain a more resourceful state within yourself.

People often fail to call for a time out, because they do not have anything else to do with their upset energy than to let it drive them into the Hole.

In & Down is a vastly preferable alternative. Practice and master this basic inner tool, and you will significantly increase your ability to be effective in relationships.

CHAPTER NINE

COMMUNICATE TO GET POSITIVE RESULTS

"Two monologs do not make a dialog."—JEFF DALY

If you want to communicate well, you need to be in a resourceful state. This is especially true when you are dealing with problems, differences and potentially charged issues.

The bottom line is that it is your job to be heard.

If you have an important message, you want it to be heard and understood.

Your style of delivery of that message, and the context in which it is given, will make all the difference.

This chapter is about setting up a context for productive communication. We will look at a specific set of tools for how to have an effective conversation.

The process of communicating involves two people. We can easily forget this. We usually see communication only from our own point of view. We know what we mean to say, and it's our partner's job to understand us.

A grammarian fell into a well one day and had difficulty climbing up the slippery sides. A little later, a Sufi chanced by and heard the man's cries for succor. In the casual language of everyday life, the Sufi offered aid.

The grammarian replied, "I would certainly appreciate your help. But by the way, you have committed an error in your speech," which the grammarian proceeded to specify.

"A good point," acknowledged the Sufi. "I had best go off awhile and try to improve my skills." And so he did, leaving the grammarian at the bottom of the well.

Here is an important fact about communication:

The Meaning of your communication is... the Response you get!

The real message the grammarian delivered was to tell the Sufi to leave—by insulting him. Remember, it is *your* job to get your intended message across. So figure out how to express yourself so that you will be heard.

Partners often pay attention to *what* they're trying to say, rather than to *how* they say it. Hence this rule:

If you do not get the Response you want... then Do Something Different!

The Golden Rule, as always, applies.

A story of another man in the hole is warranted. All the village was gathered around the empty well, trying to get this man out before the sun went down.

They were shouting, "Give me your hand!" But the man would not respond.

Meanwhile, a Sufi came by and noticed what was going on. He made his way through the crowd, to the edge of the hole, and looked down at the man.

"What is your profession, friend?" he asked.

"I am a tax collector," gasped the man.

"Well in that case," said the Sufi, "*take* my hand!"

The man immediately reached up, took the Sufi's hand.

After he was pulled to safety, the Sufi then told the crowd:

"Never ask a tax collector to *give* you anything!"

It is your job to notice whether your intended message is getting across to your partner. Notice their response. If it is not what you intended, then respect the importance of your intention—and change *how* you are communicating.

Recall how Sarah reacted when Michael tried to lighten things up by teasing. If he stayed true to his intention and applied the Golden Rule, then he might have said, "Wow! That really upset you. I'm sorry—that wasn't my intention. Do you want to talk about it?" Then he'd just listen.

WHAT IS YOUR TRUE INTENTION?

When communicating about a difficult matter, there may be a number of competing intentions that direct your words and actions.

For instance, Michael has the intention to lighten things up in the moment when he teased Sarah. He simultaneously had an intention to share a rewarding relationship with her.

But when she blew up at him for his teasing, several other intentions arose. Feeling shocked and hurt, another aspect of him may have taken over—coping strategies under stress.

On this level, his intention was to just try to cope with the sudden onset of anxiety and upset feelings. Perhaps another part of him also jumped to cover those over quickly, to wall off any sense of vulnerability.

The intention for self-protection often comes up when we get upset in a challenging situation. Depending on personality type, this may result in our shutting down, or going on the offensive. We may freeze and get numb, or hit back.

These are all strategies of being in the Hole. They produce the very opposite of what our highest intentions are—to share authentic, open, courageous, honest, supportive love.

If Michael remembered his higher intentions, he may have been able to stop himself from going to the Hole. But most often, we lose track under the stress of internal upset.

The intentions mentioned above concern the relationship and how we interact as partners.

Even more fundamental is our own personal highest intention.

If we shift our attention within ourselves, to hold onto our highest personal intention, then we can hold onto ourselves— even as the interpersonal weather around us changes.

A storm could be brewing, a heavy downpour may have arrived—yet we can stay centered in knowing our own true highest intention.

We are speaking of intentions like "Growth" or "Healing" (Chapter 2) which represent our personal aspiration to be at our best in any situation or circumstance.

Even if your relationship has become very upsetting, even if there are presently difficult and emotionally charged issues that challenge you—can you still be in touch with a personal intention such as "Growth"?

If Michael had held onto such a clear inner intentionality, he may have remembered to go In & Down, to reach deep within himself, to hold onto himself—when Sarah blew up.

To the extent we hold onto our true intentions, we can operate at our best in any situation. Being able to recall our highest intention at any moment is critical. Only by doing that can we set our course in the direction we truly want to go.

SET YOUR INTENTION

Later in this chapter we will look at the details of a way to communicate that supports you to stay at your best.

You can use this communication tool proactively—to initiate a discussion—or as a way to continue talking after you have taken a Time Out around some topic.

In either case, it is vital to clearly set your intention before launching into a discussion of the topic at hand.

Say something like:

"My intention for this talk is growth"

Hold onto your own highest intention as you talk and listen to each other.

Before any talking starts, take a moment in silence to go inside yourself and get in touch with this intention. Specifically go In & Down (Chapter 8), deep within yourself, and as you breathe, fill yourself with the desire for "Growth" or whatever word expresses your higher intention (Chapter 2).

Silently ask yourself, "How would I listen right now if I were fully in touch with my intention for growth?" Before you talk, ask yourself, "How would I say this if I were speaking in a way that represents personal growth?"

Pay attention to the answers you get inside—they may guide you to do something constructive, from the best in you. You may not feel comfortable. But remember, discomfort is often a sign you are going down a new road!

Once you have ahold of your higher intention, there are several new things you might do to support it.

NEW COMMUNICATION OPTIONS

- Talker-Listener tool
- Short durations (5 minutes)
- Create safety (vs. fixing things)
- Really listen (vs. figuring it out)
- Be resourceful (go In & Down)
- Claim your baggage
- Do an emotional transformation process
- Get support from a third party
- "Time Out" if what you do doesn't work, and then Do Something Different!

TALKER-LISTENER. One person talks, the other just listens. This is doing something different from the usual back and forth talking, where neither partner ever feels they are heard. We'll give you all the details on how to do this below. We call it the Talker-Listener tool.

SHORT DURATIONS. The goal is to stay constructive, so make your discussion brief. Limit it to five minutes. Only one person talks for that period of time. Stop and return to the topic again in an hour or two, when the other person gets their five minutes to talk.

CREATE SAFETY. Keep your focus on how to create more safety for both of you in talking and listening. Instead of just having your "eye on the prize" of getting your point across, look at whether what you are doing is creating safety.

Talk about how to create more safety in dealing with issues. Sometime, when you are not in the Hole, ask each other, "What would create more safety for you when we discuss charged topics?"

REALLY LISTEN. Practice the art of really listening. You know you are listening when your mind is quiet, like a calm lake. No ripples. No thinking what you should say in return. Just breathe and be silent, inside as well as outside.

This is a vital skill. Without it, you have little chance of succeeding in love. With it, you are empowered to deal with a wide range of challenges in personal and professional relationships. Take every opportunity to practice it.

The Talker-Listener tool below will actually train you in this most important communication skill. Most of us think we already know how to listen. But we are actually having a lot of thoughts and feelings while silent—and that is not listening.

Shockingly, listening alone—from a place of deep silence within—is enough to resolve most interpersonal problems.

Read the last paragraph again.

Until you directly experience the power of true listening, you are blind to the most powerful tool of all.

BE RESOURCEFUL. Couples often react as they try to solve an issue. They get lost in their storyline, and forget to stay resourceful. This can easily take them to the Hole.

So keep your eye on the real prize, not just the issue of the day. The real prize is to be a resourceful communicator.

Before you start talking or listening, spend five minutes going In & Down to get centered.

As you engage in communicating, maintain your calm, centered state. Continue to move your awareness In & Down throughout the process. Staying In & Down will help keep you from becoming reactive and going to the Hole.

CLAIM BAGGAGE. Every time you discuss a charged issue, it is a good opportunity to go to the Baggage Claim Area. We covered this extensively in prior chapters. We will follow with more examples.

EMOTIONAL TRANSFORMATION. Go beyond the current topic and heal old wounds. Use the currently charged feelings and engage in a process to transform your negative emotions. We present such a process in the next chapter.

GET THIRD PARTY HELP. If you don't seem to be able to go anywhere but the Hole, seek guidance from a third party. It seems impossible at times to be constructive. A third party can see options neither of you can see when you in the Hole.

The third party can be a wise friend or a professional counselor. If you truly wish to improve your resources and communication skills, remember the value of third party guidance. There is no quicker way to learn to do something different than getting a view of how someone else, who is not charged up by your topic, would address the challenge.

TIME OUT. If what you are doing does not work, and you are moving to the Hole again, go ahead and call "Time Out" again. This is a fundamental skill. The Time Out agreement is always in effect.

A POWERFUL TOOL

Starting on the next page, you will see the Talker-Listener tool in detail. This is a key tool that is the centerpiece of this book. It will increase your effectiveness in communication like nothing else, and help you maximize positive results.

You will have to practice this tool to master it. But consider the tool as presented to be like training wheels on a bike. Once mastered, you will be able to loosen the structure.

Remember the quote at the start of this chapter? "Two monologs do not make a dialog."

The Talker-Listener tool gets you to truly "do something different" from the usual back and forth talking, where neither partner feels heard. It stops that pattern cold.

It gives each partner the chance to feel like they are really heard. When is the last time that happened to you?

You can use this communication tool proactively, when there is something on your mind or in your feelings. Instead of avoiding it, initiate a Talker-Listener to create the safe space to bring it out in the open and discuss it.

Simply tell your partner, "I have something to discuss. When would you be able to do a Talker-Listener?" Let them set the time, whether they can do it immediately or schedule it within the next 24 hours.

The other way to use this communication tool is when you have had to take a Time Out. When you get back together, use Talker-Listener as a way you to address the topic that proved challenging. Whoever called Time Out takes the role of listener when you return to the topic. Note, you may sometimes feel it more appropriate to do it the other way around.

TALKER - LISTENER TOOL

The following elements are the most important in the Talker-Listener tool:

- **Listener sets when to do the session**
- **Session duration is 5 minutes**
- **Start by going In & Down for 30 seconds**
- **Each of you state your highest intention**
- **Don't switch roles for at least an hour**
- **If returning from a Time Out period, the listener is whoever said "Time Out"**

1. The Listener is in charge of scheduling when a Talker-Listener session will happen. The Listener takes responsibility to show up in a resourceful state. Only they can say when they can show up that way. Honor the work required to get resourceful. Always let the one who will next take the role of Listener set the time for the next Talker-Listener session.

2. The duration of a Talker-Listener session is 5 minutes. It is not an open-ended discussion. Beware of longer durations.

3. Start by taking 30 seconds to go In & Down (Chapter 8) and get centered. This is a vital key to being resourceful.

4. Then each of you state your highest personal intention. Keep it short, like, "My intention for this talk is Growth." The Listener says it first, as the only thing they say. Then the Talker will start their talk by stating their intention.

5. When 5 minutes is up, sit in silence for a couple of minutes. Then don't switch roles for at least an hour. After the Talker finishes speaking take at least an hour automatic Time Out. Wait at least 60 minutes before the Listener becomes the next Talker, and speaks for their 5 minutes. Again, let the next Listener set exactly when the next session will happen.

6. If this is a proactive Talker-Listener, then the one who requested the session is the Talker, and the other is the Listener. If, however, you are returning from a Time Out period, the Listener is whoever called for the time out. Remember, the translation of "Time Out" is "Let's return to this later, when I'll be resourceful enough to hear you." So if you call Time Out, your job is to come back and be a resourceful Listener.

THE ROLE OF LISTENER — BE QUIET

- Center yourself, breathe, go In & Down
- Silently hold your highest intention
- Don't be reactive, dodge all arrows
- Say "Time Out" again if reacting

The Listener's job is to hear what the other person says. They are silent on the inside and outside. So if you are the Listener, you need to develop these skills:

1. Pay attention to your breath. Keep breathing. Go In & Down (Chapter 8). Be centered. Feel your feet on the floor, contacting the earth below. Just relax. Really sit in your chair. Remember, there's nothing to think, say or do here.

2. Silently hold your highest intention (Chapter 2). If it is "Growth," then sense how you are growing right now as your partner speaks. Don't try to figure it out. Just see it that way. See an alternative version of you and your partner where you both are growing. Keep that image alive in your mind's eye.

3. If you feel yourself react, remember your breath and let go of the energy of reacting. Breathe it out. Go deeply In & Down on your next breath. Or pretend you are dodging arrows, a spiritual exercise of sorts. What your partner says might seem like an arrow coming at you. That is just an illusion, it's only your imagination. Let it fly right by. There's nothing you have to do about it. Don't grab onto the arrow. Don't jump in front of it. Stop yourself from making your own point. A point is at the tip of an arrow, and it can only hurt you!

4. If you do slip up and grab onto an arrow and start to inflict it upon yourself, you may react instead of listening. That's a signal for you to say "Time Out" and reschedule for later, when you can just listen to and hear your partner.

Here's a story of a great warrior. Though quite old, the warrior still was able to defeat any challenger. His reputation spread far and wide throughout the land and many students gathered to study under him.

One day a young warrior arrived. He was determined to be the first man to defeat the great master. Along with his strength, he had an uncanny ability to spot and exploit any weakness in an opponent.

He would wait for his opponent to make the first move,

thus revealing a weakness. Then he would hit with merciless force and lightning speed. No one had ever lasted with him in a match beyond the first move.

Much against the advice of his concerned students, the old master gladly accepted the young warrior's challenge. As the two squared off for battle, the young warrior began to hurl insults at the old master. He threw dirt and spit in his face. For hours he verbally assaulted him with every curse and insult known to mankind. But the old warrior merely stood there motionless and calm. Finally, the young warrior exhausted himself. Knowing he was defeated, he left feeling shamed.

Somewhat disappointed that he did not fight the insolent youth, the students gathered around the old master and questioned him. "How could you endure such an indignity? How did you drive him away?"

"If someone comes to give you a gift and you do not receive it," the master said, "to whom does the gift belong?"

The famous anthropologist Gregory Bateson[2], an authority on world cultures and languages, made the following profound observation about communication. He studied cultures and languages around the world. He observed that people are saying one of two things at all times, no matter what the topic or what the words.

It doesn't matter if people are in a third-world village talking about chickens and cows, or if they are on Wall Street discussing stocks and bonds. People are always saying one of two basic things.

People are either saying they are reasonably content—or that they are upset. The words and story are secondary to this underlying message.

WATCH THE VOLCANO

As a Listener there's an inner image that might help you in staying centered. Imagine a volcano releasing its energy. You don't want to plug up a volcano. Just ask a geologist.

Likewise, it's not very productive to interfere when your partner is releasing their steam. Don't try to make sense of, fix, or change what your partner is saying—or feeling. Don't try to talk them out of it or take it on yourself. Don't correct their words or story.

Even with the most helpful of intentions, doing any of those things interfere with your partner's process. It's like putting a plug in the volcano. It won't work!

All you have to do is watch—and dodge whatever seems to be coming at you. There's really nothing else you *can* do. That is the wisdom of watching the volcano.

When the volcano emits gas, fire, lava, smoke or ash—it is releasing pressures you don't want to block or let build up further. This is a natural process.

In relationship, as emotions are released, the presence of a partner who is truly listening can lead to a great inner healing. Trying to block this release, by not listening or otherwise interrupting your partner will only lead to bigger blowups down the road.

Encourage your partner to express all they need to release. It clears the way for better communication later. The wisdom is to stay centered and listen—and not react yourself.

Call a "Time Out" if you start to react.

Being a good Listener is absolutely crucial.

THE ROLE OF TALKER — BE CONSTRUCTIVE

- FACTS — factual, non-debatable data.
- FEELINGS — actual emotions
- FUTURE — request what works for you
- FREEDOM — claim and heal your baggage
- NO FICTION — blame, interpretation

The Talker's job is to communicate in a way their partner can hear. This means being as constructive as possible under the circumstances, and honoring your highest intentions.

Ideally, we would already know how to express ourselves in a constructive way. But the reality is that we don't.

This is a skill that can be learned and refined. It is "doing something different" when talking about a charged topic. Awkward at first, it's all a matter of practice.

When you are Talker, follow a map of what to talk about, and what not to bring up. Differentiate fact from fiction, and you will be more effective.

As Talker, stick to discussing the Four F's—Facts, Feelings, Future and Freedom.

Leave out and do not discuss the Fifth F, the deadly one, the one that kills communication—Fiction.

1. FACTS — Briefly describe what you saw and heard in a specific event which gave rise to the problem you experience. If you are trying to deal with a general issue, stop generalizing and limit your discussion to a specific, concrete example.

Be specific and exactly factual. Describe the actions or words a videotape would show. Facts are non-debatable.

Example: "We agreed to meet for dinner at six. You arrived at seven."

All facts. Nothing can be debated by either party. This simple way of talking works better than the kind of complex and accusatory statements we usually make.

2. FEELINGS — Say what feeling you had. Limit yourself to actual feelings, not interpretive judgments about the other person and the quality of their actions.

Actual feelings are simple and direct: anger, hurt, sad, afraid, fear, anxiety, frustration, irritation, confused. These are descriptions of what is taking place inside of you.

Example: "I felt hurt." "I felt angry."

Keep it simple and clear. Keep it totally about your own inner emotional state.

3. FUTURE — Make a specific request about what might work better for you in the future. Be concrete in terms of what you would see or hear. Our example above: "You were an hour

late. I felt hurt." Continuing, your request might be: "In the future, it would work better for me if you could call me if you know you might be more than ten minutes late."

4. FREEDOM — Go to the Baggage Claim Area. Use the upset feelings that are coming up to direct you towards the 95% factor that is kicking in. This creates better understanding and supports healing. We'll discuss this in detail below.

5. NO FICTION — When we interpret or judge others, we are making up our own fictional account of what happened. When we label or name call, it is a fictional characterization of another human. When we attribute blame to one person, it is also complete fiction.

Fiction only leads to friction.

Do not include judgment, name calling, or interpreting of your partner's actions. Don't just dump your feelings on your partner in the form of blaming them for how you feel.

That will only take both of you to the Hole.

We all will tend to automatically interpret a situation in terms of how our partner acted or made us feel. We ascribe certain explanations that paint them negatively.

Some examples: "You were disrespectful!" or "It was insensitive of you to be late."

Interpretations cleverly disguise themselves. We generally think we are stating facts or feelings. But do you really know the difference between facts, feelings and interpretations?

Fiction creates friction. Being interpreted is offensive. You only ruin communication—and dampen love—when you state your judgments and fictional interpretations.

FACTS AND FEELINGS — NOT FICTION

State Facts and Feelings. Say only factual, non-debatable things. Most often this is a factual description of a specific behavior of your partner and the specific emotion you felt.

Here are some examples:

- "You were 60 minutes late. I felt hurt."
- "You told them my secret. I feel sad."
- "You didn't thank me for cooking. I feel upset."
- "You didn't wash dishes as agreed. I feel angry."

Talk about one specific event rather than discussing many events over time. You describe the actions a videotape would show—without interpreting the behavior.

The Feeling you mention is a specific emotional state, like "anger" "hurt" "sad" "upset" or "afraid."

Say what was said or done, and the emotion you felt. Say it as a weather report, not as an attack or judgment.

Leaving out your Fiction can be a discipline at first.

We are blind to how much interpretation and judgment we routinely do. Here are the above examples—contaminated with added judgments, turned into destructive Fiction:

- "You were inconsiderately late!"
- "You have such a big mouth!"
- "You take me for granted!"
- "You're so irresponsible, just like a little boy!"

When someone hears such judgments, they get defensive.

A judgment is your opinion, your interpretation of the facts. By not sticking to non-debatable facts, you offend the Listener and push both of you into the Hole.

Remember, Fiction creates friction.

Watch out when you state the Feeling, too.

This often gets contaminated with judgment. People think a Feeling is anything that starts with the words "I feel..."

Wrong! Here are the second parts of the examples, turned into Fiction by judgment:

- "I feel you are rude and inconsiderate!"
- "I feel betrayed!"
- "I feel unappreciated!"
- "I feel a lack of sincerity here!"

These are not Feelings at all. For instance, "You are rude" is a judgment of the other person. It is not an emotion. Neither is "unappreciated!" It's a guess about what the other person is thinking about you. It is all just Fiction.

To state a Feeling, choose from the following words: "angry" "hurt" "sad" "upset" or "afraid."

Another contamination is to imply your partner "causes" what you feel. Examples:

- "You made me angry when you were late!"
- "You were late and that made me angry!"
- "I'm so hurt because you were late!"

This is just more Fiction, another form of blame. It only takes both of you deep into the Hole.

FUTURE — MAKE A REQUEST

State a specific action you want your partner to consider doing in the Future.

This is only a request. They have the right to say no.

A request can be part of a Talker-Listener. It can also be the only thing you have to say.

Here are examples of requests that build on the statements in the last section. They all start with the words, "It would work better for me in the future if you..."

- "Call me if you are going to be late."
- "Keep my secrets totally to yourself."
- "Say 'Thanks' if I do the cooking."
- "Honor your agreement and wash the dishes."

A request is very clear, simple and direct.

If all you want to do is make a request, start with the words, "I have a request. Please..." then make the request, "...call me if you are going to be late." Keep it short, simple and non-judgmental.

You will contaminate a request by slipping a judgment in. For instance, "I have a request. Please be more considerate in the future. Call me if you will be late." The middle sentence is name calling. Your partner will be offended or get defensive instead of hearing and responding to your request.

Avoid setting off on a trip to the Hole. If your request is important enough for you to have strong feelings, then it deserves to be delivered in a way your partner can hear it and be able to respond to it. As Talker, the delivery is your job.

THE CHALLENGE —
TO DEVELOP YOUR SKILL

Most of us get caught up in the *story* of what "makes" us upset. We try to communicate this to our partner, in hopes that they will hear us, understand and respond.

Unfortunately, we don't pay as close attention to *how* we are communicating our important message. Sometimes we resemble the grammarian in the hole who corrected the Sufi's syntax. We are like that when we just want to get the facts right, to correct our partner in some way. The usual result is that partners get defensive, we are not heard—and everyone ends up going to the Hole together.

Beyond any particular issue that may challenge you, the real challenge is to develop skills in delivering your message. Otherwise you are doomed to keep trying to work things out in the same old way, and end up in the same old place.

As Talker, give as much attention to *how* you express yourself, as you give to the content of the storyline of the day. Keep free of judgment or blame. Use short sentences and talk about specific actions or feelings. Make specific requests. Move on from there to explore the opportunity for personal growth or healing that can come of the situation.

As Listener, give as much attention to how resourceful and present you can be, as you give to the words in the storyline. Do not fall for judgments or try to change your partner's ideas or feelings. Just listen and do nothing.

No matter what the current storyline, the real challenge in relationship is to learn to do something different, to develop new skills and to travel on a new road together.

FREEDOM — HEALING PAST BAGGAGE

A way to be free of past baggage is to consciously realize how it affects your emotional reactions in the present.

Explore the affects of your past when you are the Talker. Doing this can be a path to personal growth and healing.

We call this going to the Baggage Claim Area.

WELCOME TO THE BAGGAGE CLAIM AREA

PLEASE PROCEED WITH CARE:

1. LOCATE EACH OF THE PIECES
2. IDENTIFY OWNERSHIP
3. OPEN & EXAMINE CONTENTS

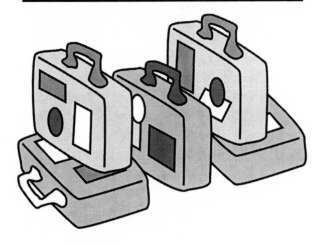

When you choose to go the the Baggage Claim Area, it helps to defuse a situation. It assists you to make better sense of all the feelings that are coming up.

By linking charged feelings you have now to events that happened to you in the past, you can discover and heal old wounds. In the short run, it may seem unnecessary and very difficult to do this. But in the long run, it will lead you to share a greater understanding with your partner and can reduce the amount of suffering you encounter.

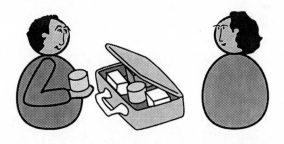

Here are some ways to begin talking about the past factor of your present feelings:

- "What's coming up for me from my past is..."
- "This is like when I was young and..."
- "This is a familiar feeling. It reminds me of when..."

Here is how that might sound. "You were late. I felt hurt. It reminded me of when I was young and my father would promise to pick me up after school and then be an hour late... or even forget to pick me up..."

Tell your partner the whole story of the past. Share what

adds in to your upset today. "It led me to think he just didn't care... and I felt a sense of being abandoned. This seems to come up now for me when someone is late..."

You might even decide how to refer to this sensitivity. Maybe call it "my abandonment thing." This will help both of you to identify it in the future and not mistake the feelings that are coming up as just about the present topic.

Understanding each other's past baggage and 95% factors can help couples do things differently. Partners will better respect each others' sensitivities. They make positive changes in how they act and communicate with each other.

CLAIM BAGGAGE AND HEAL

You can claim and heal past baggage as a conscious choice, not just as a part of doing the Talker-Listener tool.

The act of claiming baggage is as simple as telling stories. The stories relate what it was like to grow up in your family. Give your partner a chance to understand what your past was like and how it influenced you.

Discuss only what you are comfortable to reveal.

Talk about the communication styles that you learned in your family. Point out the patterns you have recognized in yourself and how far back they go. Look at any sensitivities that may have come out of that early experience.

A good time to share baggage is when you are challenged by someone other than your partner. Describe to your partner what concerns you have with that other person. Then let your mind wander, and fill in the following sentence:

"This reminds me of when I was young, and..."

Tell a story about what the current situation resembles in your past. Explore what might be coming up from that past: some old pattern, hot button, sensitivity or wound.

Research shows that a major factor in great relationships is that each partner understands the sensitivities of the other person. Sharing your stories builds this understanding.

HOW TO FIND LOST BAGGAGE

Sometimes it is hard to immediately see what is affecting you from your past. If this is difficult to do, try the following exercise to explore your past.

Think of any recent upsetting feeling you had.

In your mind's eye, visualize the event that triggered this feeling in you. See whatever you saw at the time, until you start to feel the upset feeling.

Now hold onto the feeling, and let go of the event.

Start to imagine you are back in your childhood home. You are younger than sixteen, say. Maybe even younger than ten years old.

Look for a time when you felt a similar upset feeling.

Just observe whatever comes up.

It may be a specific event—or a composite of many events. Whatever comes is okay. Just go with it.

If you prefer a little emotional distance, watch the event as an outside observer would view it. Watch as if you were a visitor who has come to help this young person out—to free them. Send that young person your love and support.

When you finish watching, if you feel up to it, explore if there is another key event at an earlier age.

WHEN TO CLAIM BAGGAGE

When do you visit the Baggage Claim Area? Consider it a gradual and ongoing process. It is good to set it in motion from the start of a significant relationship. But don't overdo it. Don't start it prematurely, like telling all about your deepest wounds and fears on your very first date.

On the other hand, it's never too late. We have witnessed couples married for thirty years begin to claim baggage, and deep healing and understanding resulted. Years of upsets and issues can be healed in a short time, when partners let down the defenses and claim their baggage together.

Consider the story of the old farmer and the rock. He'd plowed around a large rock in one of his fields for year after year. He had broken several plows on the rock and had grown rather morbid about it over time.

After breaking another plow, and remembering all the trouble the rock had caused him through the years, he finally decided to do something about it.

When he put his crowbar under it, he was very surprised to discover that the rock was only about six inches thick and that he could break it up easily with a hammer. As he was carting the pieces away he had to smile, remembering all the trouble that the rock had caused him over the years and how easy it would have been to deal with it sooner.

It is always a good time to start the process of claiming baggage. Do it when you feel resourceful. If you are upset, it may not be the best time to try to share baggage. Of course, when you are very upset, it is not a good time to even try to communicate.

BENEFITS OF CLAIMING BAGGAGE

- Leads to healing and wholeness
- The 95% factor is reduced
- Upsets can be diminished
- Perspective is increased
- Your relationships stay clear

Wise partners know that claiming baggage is an important step towards healing and wholeness.

When you think your upsets are solely caused by others, you are disconnected from the part within yourself that reacts—a part that may be mirrored by the other person. At the Baggage Claim Area, you open things up to name and discover more parts of yourself.

This is an act of ownership and reconnection. To the extent it is done in a safe and loving context, healing can happen. That is why the agreements you make with your partner around claiming baggage are so very important.

As baggage is claimed you can see more clearly when stuff from the past—the 95% factor—kicks into any current situation. By seeing this, it has less power. When stuff from the past has less power, you are freed from acting out conflict with each other. You spend less time being upset, and more time being loving and constructive.

More situations that normally lead to the Hole will be manageable as a result of claiming baggage. You will have greater perspective and will be able to create agreements rather than spinning around the vicious circle, down the spiral, and into the Hole.

PLAY AN ACTIVE ROLE

Claiming baggage is a major step that says, "Okay, I am a part of what goes on after all." Done in the spirit of improving things, this will empower both you and your partner to actively change what is going on.

Always remember to claim baggage in the spirit of mutually improving things. Beware of falling back into the unconscious pattern of assigning blame, of saying, "See, it's your problem after all!" It's not about finding fault.

When you claim baggage, you see your patterns. You recognize emotional triggers. You admit sensitivities. You own hot buttons. You can name how your old wounds are restimulated. You see the role your family conditioning plays. You admit limiting beliefs or communication styles.

At first, this might not seem like a path to empowerment. It is uncomfortable to open up, explore and name such things to your partner. It may even seem like you have to give up necessary power or defensive ability.

But when you let yourself believe it's all their fault, you severely limit your own options. You have no power to heal or change. It will take an act of waking up to really transform a relationship, or your life. Claiming baggage is an important part of this waking up.

BEGIN THE PROCESS NOW

If you are in a relationship, we recommend you discuss with your partner the contents of this chapter. If you are single, do this with a willing friend, family member or relative.

Create an agreement to use the Talker-Listener tool and to claim baggage in the spirit of positive transformation, rather than finding fault. Discuss what would create safety for each of you.

Do this exercise. Choose a recent event where you got mildly upset with someone. Mild is 3 on a scale of 10. Recall the event in your mind's eye. Watch the event as if you are viewing a videotape. Then write the following information on a sheet of paper.

1. <u>Facts</u>: Briefly describe exactly what you saw and heard in that situation. Be specific and factual. Describe only actions or words a videotape would show. This can include gestures and voicetones.

2. <u>Feelings</u>: What was the emotional state you felt? Write "I felt ____." Then fill in the emotion. Use a simple word like: "angry" "frustrated" "irritated" "afraid" "anxious" "hurt" "sad"

3. <u>Fiction</u>: Write down your judgments. How do you interpret the other person's acts? What negative label would you put on them? This is all the stuff to leave out of a Talker-Listener. Write it down here, so you know what not to say.

4. <u>Future</u>: What would work for you better in the future in terms of specific words and actions? Be clear. Write exactly what a videotape would show.

5. Freedom: Write what the situation reminds you of from your past. Imagine you are back in your childhood home. Find a situation back then when you felt a similar upset feeling. Whatever comes is okay. Watch it as if you are seeing a videotape.

You are now prepared with the data for a Talker-Listener session. If you were going to actually do a session, you might initiate it the following way:

"I have something I'd like to talk about. Is there a time I could talk and you could just listen for five minutes?"

Some people just say, "I'd like to do a Talker-Listener."

Let the other person specify when they can do it.

When you start the session, go In & Down for at least 30 seconds to center yourselves.

Then the Listener says their highest positive intention. Then you state yours, like "My intention for this is personal growth and healing."

Now you have 5 minutes as Talker. Read what you wrote for Facts, Feelings, Future and Freedom.

Do not include Fiction. It only creates friction.

When you are done, say "Thanks for listening."

Tell them when you will be available to listen to them in the next session, if there needs to be one. Take at least an hour break before changing roles.

A series of Talker-Listener sessions may be called for, in order to reach a mutual creative solution.

Or maybe just one person listening to the other is all that needed to happen.

CHAPTER TEN

TRANSFORM NEGATIVE FEELINGS

*"You must be the change you wish
to see in the world."*—GANDHI

When a relationship is "good" you are moving with full sails ahead. The sky is sunny, waters are smooth. Everything is ship shape. It's a time of joy and positive feelings.

- **Sunny skies**
- **Smooth sailing**
- **Everything's ship shape**

These are times in relationship when our hearts open and we feel expansive and uplifted. Many people define having a good relationship to be a function of the presence of positive feelings—and the absence of negative ones.

An upset-avoidant couple's motto is:

Just be sure not to "Rock the Boat!"

Being in an upset-avoidant framework, a relationship can appear to be going okay. Partners can take pride that they never fight. They may put their attention on matters external to the relationship itself, such as childraising, homemaking, career, business, whatever.

But in avoiding their potential to feel "bad," they also limit their potential to feel anything—including "good." Relationships in a state of avoidance can die of boredom.

True harmony cannot come from avoiding things. If you find yourself in such a limbo state, it's a signal that this is the time to learn and expand your relating skills.

The right relating skills can make all the difference. Without these skills, deeper emotions and conflict will lead to destructive behavior. With these skills, however, you will find healing, a deeper connection and stronger passion.

Are your maintaining an apparent state of harmony at all costs? Or can you afford to rock the boat a little, as a part of moving forward?

You don't really achieve anything by not rocking the boat, other than to let things build up under the surface, not faced and not dealt with. Such things will ultimately come to the surface later, with far more force and power.

Then the relationship can suddenly seem to be "bad." Just as sudden as an unforecasted storm. The waters are choppy and the sky is full of clouds—maybe thunder and lightning. The sun is hidden. You have that sinking feeling.

Often, when couples stay very upset with each other, they begin to describe the relationship as if it's a boat that has a hole in it. They may even feel like they are sinking.

- Turbulence
- Hole in the boat
- You seem to be sinking fast

As they describe what is going on, it seems like the most important question to them is figuring out who is causing the challenge they both are experiencing. Of course, each partner blames the situation on the other person.

THE BLAME GAME

A couple could focus on finding a positive solution, one which works to mutually satisfy the wants and needs that are not being met in the challenging situation. But sadly, couples usually tend to place their focus on "What is wrong?" and "Whose fault is this?"

With this usual focus, there is little energy left over for creating a solution or discovering new and possible options. Instead, partners spend all their energy in the misguided attempt to figure out who to blame the problem on.

Essentially, this is like two people in a sinking boat who are only asking one question:

Whose Side of the Boat has the Hole?

Each partner points the finger at the other. Each says it's the other person who is causing the relationship to suffer. Meanwhile this boat they call their love is going under.

Each gets trapped in the blame game instead of grabbing a bucket and starting to bail the water out. Each thinks its their partner's job to do that.

Will finding out whose side of the boat has the hole stop them from sinking? Clearly not. Does this approach work any better for relationships? No!

We have never seen that approach work, in love or at sea. In fact, this approach adds weight to the boat, or the love relationship, and makes it sink faster. Trying to determine whose side of the boat has the hole is the same as going down that same old road and falling into the Hole.

ASK BETTER QUESTIONS

Figuring out who to blame for upset in a relationship is the wrong question. It is based on the wrong assumptions. People are looking external to themselves for the Hole, when it is really something going on within each of them.

Couples can travel a new road when they realize there are better questions to ask. For instance, it will benefit you to question whether the hole is on the outside, external to you. Only when you focus more on what is coming up within yourself, will you begin to go down a new road that can lead to personal transformation, healing and wholeness.

So a better beginning question to ask is, "Where is all of this water coming from, anyway?" Is the water coming from outside—up from the ocean and down from the sky? Or is it coming from inside?

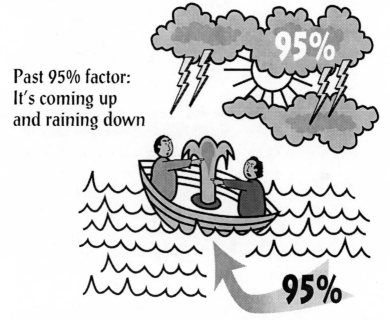

Past 95% factor: It's coming up and raining down

Better yet to ask, "Is this water entirely from the present? Or is 95% of it streaming in from the past?" When you are experiencing strong negative feelings, it is almost always the case that sensitivities from the past have kicked in.

It is important to distinguish emotions that arise based just on what is happening now in front of you—from reactions that are being amplified by your past and the 95% factor.

If you look carefully within, you will find that most of the water that rains down in emotional storms is made up of the 95% factor—unhealed wounds, emotional triggers and sensitivities from your own past.

THE BEST QUESTION

The best question of all is simply this:

What's coming up, asking for transformation?

When you ask this question, you can find answers that have the power to transform your feelings and your life.

Most of us can embrace the desire to transform and heal wounds from our past, to become more whole, and to expand beyond any negative limits set up by our past conditioning.

To do this we stop looking for solutions from our partner and we start to look within ourselves.

FOR TRANSFORMATION - LOOK INSIDE

Instead of looking outside for the source of the "Hole" in the boat, look inside to find the true source of the water.

Water is a traditional symbol for feelings. In that context, consider the following question about love and emotion....

Is the ideal love partnership like a "boat" that is supposed to insulate you from having upset feelings—just as a boat would insulate you from the dangerous waters of the ocean? And if you do start feeling upset, do you conclude the Relation Ship has a hole in it that needs to be fixed?

Most of us do, in fact, think this way. Even though the majority may do so, it does not mean it is either accurate or useful. A majority once knew the earth was flat!

This way of thinking is about blaming our partners for what we feel. We tell a story about how they made us upset, in which we usually judge them and call them names.

Instead of looking outside for the "Hole" in the boat, it's more useful to look for the source of water inside ourselves. Water springs from within us. There is no hole in the boat. And the boat is not there to keep us from the water.

Here is a little secret that runs contrary to how most of us think—or even *want* to think—about love:

Love brings up anything unlike itself... for healing and transformation

Know that deep, passionate love will naturally inspire us to move towards inner transformation, healing and wholeness. We glimpse this in the honeymoon, and start the real journey after that. The deeper the love, the more our inner darkness will rise into the light of that love.

On the journey to wholeness we will encounter things within ourselves that are not yet healed or not quite whole. Old wounds will come up to bathe in the light of love. We will run up against past wounds, old sensitivities, emotional triggers and hot buttons. We will bump into limiting negative beliefs, old programming and old patterns.

Collectively, these wounds, sensitivities, triggers, hot buttons and inner limits make up what we have been calling the "95% factor" from the past.

This is what comes up in a loving relationship. This is the source of upset. While we may initially think it's an unwanted hole in the boat letting dangerous waters from the outside in, it is really something quite different.

The waters are within us. Love sets these waters to rising. The waters arise with the intent of our finding transformation and wholeness—or whatever other word you use for it: healing, freedom, personal growth, balance, peace.

These are our highest intentions in life (Chapter 2). It is more accurate and useful for couples to see the emergence of upsets as a natural part of love. They are empowered as they consciously align themselves to their higher intentions.

They do not have to use the same word. One partner may be dedicated to "Growth" and the other senses the word "Healing" more captures their higher intention. These are all synonyms. Each helps us embrace upsets as a part of love— and see these as a very positive and natural process.

An intention like "Growth" is naming something that is already deeply important within ours souls. To name it, is to stay conscious of it and to remember that transformation is a part of the loving journey. Remembering our personal higher intention keeps love afloat when the waters start to rise!

Transformation is a process of moving from the "Hole" to wholeness.

Think of transformation as the flowing of the inner waters towards the ocean of wholeness.

Instead of going to the Hole or thinking there's a hole in the boat, we can learn to just let the water flow through us. We don't have to block the water or build a defensive dam.

Most of us are so used to thinking of upset emotions as a hole in the boat, that the idea of transformation or wholeness may seem not only foreign, but unreachable.

It takes conscious effort to think in a new way and do something different. There are big rewards for making the effort to think differently about love and upset.

We encourage you to face the awkwardness, summon the courage, and make this effort. Remember, it takes conscious effort to move down a new road.

The road we are describing is real—and you can travel it. It is a road taken by wise partners. It is a road where challenges and upsets are embraced, where partners heal and become more whole, where love grows stronger as a result.

TRANSFORMATION — A DIFFERENT ROAD

It's an inner journey—a flow of transforming energy through the self—supported by your highest intentions.

You can choose to see upsets in relationship as occasions for inner transformation. The shift happens inside yourself. We will use the word "transformation" to refer to this inner shift. Feel free to use a different word, one that matches your personal highest intentions. Whatever word you use, you are choosing to transform all that blocks you inside, from fully experiencing and expressing love.

Transformation can be experienced as a flow of energy through ourselves. The special energies of the honeymoon period are connected to this flow. Honeymoon energies are highly charged energies that are positive and magical.

The energies that flow in transformation are also highly charged. But we often label them negative and undesirable. So we block or stop the energy. We stay in our heads and become very mental. We try to turn the energy into words.

What we do is tell a story about what's wrong, who is to blame for it, and why it's such a bad thing. Sometimes the story is an attempt to fix or repair things.

What is missing in story-telling is to directly experience

the energy that corresponds to our emotions. Perhaps this is protective, because we don't think we can truly bear feeling the feelings. Or maybe we truly believe we can solve things on a verbal level—by talking and talking.

Whatever the motivation, we end up keeping our focus *above* the neck, in our heads—which in essence, insulates us from the flow of the waters. Unfortunately, this insulation acts like a dam, blocking the flow of our energy.

So the emotional energy underlying our "problems" is never released or transformed. It tends to stick around, build up—even clog up our ability to feel much love after awhile. We keep having the same discussions, over and over again. Then we wonder why our issues never seem to resolve.

We don't resolve these issues because we don't transform the energies *below* our neck. These unresolved emotions add into our accumulated baggage, our 95% factor—which in turn increases how upset we will get in the future.

The solution is to move our focus into the body. When we directly work with the energy below the neck, we can move towards transformation and wholeness.

We will now offer you a process for doing this, one that you can do with a partner or alone. Doing it as a solo process is discussed at the end of the chapter. We start by showing you how to do it with a partner.

FLOW THROUGH PROCESS

We call this process Flow Through because it feels like a flow of energy through the body, a flow that results in a sense of deep inner transformation.

Do a Flow Through if you want to transform—rather than talk about—emotional upset. This process heals old baggage carried around from the past, your 95% factor. It is a process to do something different, to transform your charged energies—rather than going to the Hole or getting into a stuck space.

In the Flow Through process, each partner has a distinct role. The role of the supportive partner is called "Witness." And the role of the active partner who is going to transform their emotional state is called "Flow Through."

Flow Through　　　**Witness**

95%

We will look at each role in detail. This process can take 30 to 60 minutes in all. Most of the time, you will schedule it for a time and place that works for both partners.

Couples will often be inspired to set up a Flow Through process when one person has called a "Time Out" At that time, it may occur to either partner to invite a transformation process rather than come back and just talk about the event.

Typical invitations may sound like the following:

"I'd like to do a Flow Through with this upset. Are you willing to Witness?"

"Are you interested in doing a Flow Through around your feelings? I'm willing to Witness."

"After you said 'Time Out' I realized my upset had more to do with old baggage than with what happened here. I'd like to schedule a Flow Through. Are you available to be Witness anytime in the next few days?"

We will now examine each role, starting with Witness:

THE ROLE OF WITNESS

- **It's a choice**
- **Stay centered and breathe**
- **Hold your highest intentions**
- **Ask about body sensations**

The role of Witness is a *choice*, and a gift to your partner. You are called on to be skillful and resourceful. So your first job as Witness is to schedule the Flow Through at a time and place where you will be resourceful.

Witnessing allows your partner to move through feelings to their own natural completion. It supports them to release upset, and creates a context for transformation to happen.

To witness your partner is to be available, centered, and compassionate. It calls upon you to be nonjudgmental and noninterfering. This will be deeply appreciated.

Many of the skills of Listener are called for when you choose the role of Witness. Let's start by summarizing the major skills involved:

1. STAY CENTERED. As Witness, you are centered and quiet within yourself. You keep breathing. You are aware that your feet are in contact with the earth. You let go of any reactions that come up within yourself, and just stay present with your partner.

2. HOLD YOUR HIGHER INTENTION. In your role as Witness, hold your higher intention (Chapter 2), and keep moving your own energies toward it. Visualize "Growth" or "Healing" happening. This adds in a specific positive energy on your part to support the transformation.

3. ASK ABOUT SENSATIONS. Unlike the role of Listener, here you get to speak a bit. You will ask your partner very simple questions about what is going on inside of them. These questions will be phrased in terms of the sensations they are aware of in their body. This helps them to focus on the Flow Through process. We will discuss all this in detail.

STAY CENTERED

As a part of transformation, your partner may feel highly charged emotions. You know, those things we normally try to avoid! So your own reactions might kick in.

If your partner feels an emotion like anger, hurt, fear, or sadness, how do you typically respond? Do you withdraw, reason with them, or take on their feelings? Do you try to fix them or make them feel better? What if they seem to blame you for how they feel? Do you end up getting defensive?

None of this really works for transformation.

To be Witness, we move beyond whatever reactions we typically have. We need to put aside whatever keeps us from holding the clear vision and energy of transformation.

Examples are:

- **Feeling it's our fault**
- **Getting defensive**
- **Taking on our partner's feelings**
- **Wanting them to feel different**
- **Trying to fix them**
- **Pulling away from them**

Each of those reactions is a signal to breathe in fresh air, and breathe out whatever is coming up. The job of Witness is to stay clear and quiet within.

Go In & Down. Take full, regular breaths. Be sure to keep breathing. Feel yourself solidly connected with the earth. Let your mind be quiet and still, like a tranquil lake.

If thoughts or judgments begin to surface, simply put them

aside, and bring your focus back to your partner. If you have an urge to take care of their feelings or if you start to feel emotions yourself, breathe deeply, let go, allow it to pass through you.

It's more important to stay clear, centered and available. If you cannot do this—take Time Out. Return to the process later. This is a major skill. It takes practice.

HOLD THE HIGHEST INTENTION

As Witness, it's your job to hold sight of your higher intentions (Chapter 2). Keep alive the sense of how it gives meaning to what you are doing together right now.

Do not make the mistake of taking anything your partner says personally. Instead, see your partner as simply releasing emotional energy through their words. Allow them to release that energy. Realize that they cannot be rational right now, and that what they say may not be accurate. This is part of the process.

It may help you to know that they are releasing energy from their past—feelings that have been locked up inside since childhood, a previous relationship, or earlier in your relationship. Wherever this energy is coming from, while it remains unreleased it affects both of you, building up power as long as it stays locked inside.

As Witness, see that, at long last, this may be a moment of great transformation. The best support you can give them in their transformation is to just let your partner feel whatever comes up. Trying to fix them or make them feel better only interrupts the transformation process.

Give them a rare gift that can really help them to heal, your absolute presence. Know that they themselves have the power to release and transform. Your presence is all that's needed to support them in moving through their darkness.

SEE THE SUN RISE

It is helpful to practice the following visualization:
Imagine the sun above as you sit with your partner.
Even in the middle of the night, you know the sun still exists. It may be a dark hour emotionally, yet you know for sure the sun will rise again. There may be clouds covering it, even the rain of tears or anger, but the sun still exists.

Imagine a globe of golden sunlight filling your chest. Feel its warmth. Feel it expanding from your heart, sending its rays of light out to your partner.
Then start to imagine how they will appear when their own

sun finally rises fully within them! Even if they seem to be going through highly charged feelings, imagine in your mind's eye how they will look when their own sun rises inside of them.

See that golden globe filling their chest. Sense how it is connected with the golden warm sunlight that so easily keeps pouring out of your chest, like a cup that flows over, and keeps flowing without beginning or end.

ASK ABOUT BODY SENSATIONS

As Witness, you can speak to your partner. You ask them basic questions about the sensations they have in their body. The intent of this is to support them to stay focused on their Flow Through process.

Body sensations are the building blocks of emotions. They are the elemental components of feelings. When we move our awareness to this elemental level, the energies of emotion become more free to flow and change.

When we focus on the whole emotion, we usually say something like, "I am upset and angry!" Then we usually jump to the next thing, which is to tell the reasons and story of why we are upset and angry. The feeling itself tends to get locked in, blocked from flowing or changing.

However, when we move our awareness to the elemental level of body sensations, we might say something like, "I have a knot in my stomach" and then focus on what is happening in our body. We may report, "It is really tight."

As we pay even closer attention on this level, we will notice new things and can experience a flow of energy within ourselves. In moving our focus to this deep level of inner awareness, deep transformation can occur.

When you are being the Witness, part of your job is to help your partner stay focused on the elemental level of body sensations. You are asking your partner to describe what is going on inside of them in a specific way. Pretend there is an object inside them and you are playing "20 Questions" to figure out what it is.

Here are some guidelines for how you ask questions:

- **Be curious**
- **Talk gently**
- **Go slowly**
- **Wait a minute between questions**
- **Every question need not be answered**

The following is a set of questions you can ask. The set of questions works as a cycle that is repeated many times. These questions are simple, and have only to do with what your partner is directly experiencing in their body.

THE QUESTIONS

At the start of each set of questions ask, "What sensations are you aware of in your body right now?"

If your partner is aware of more than one sensation, ask them to choose one they want to focus on—perhaps to focus on the strongest one.

Once they have chosen the sensation they want to focus on, you will ask about various properties of that sensation.

Go slowly. Give them at least 15 seconds to answer each question. This helps them slow down and get more fully in touch with their sensations. Some questions may not get an answer. That's okay—just move on to another question.

"What is the location of this sensation in your body?"
"How big is it?"
"Does it have a shape?"
"Do you notice its weight? Is it light or heavy?"
"Do you notice its temperature? Is it warm or cool?"
"Do you notice its density? Is it solid, fluid or gas?"
"Does it have any pressure with it?"
"Is it stationary or moving?"
If it is moving, ask, "Is it just moving back and forth—or in a specific direction?" and, "How fast is it moving?"
"What is the texture of its surface? Smooth or rough?"
"Is there any color associated with it?"

The final question in the set is:

"Are you willing to just sit with this a few moments more? Know there's nothing to say, nothing to do, nothing to fix—and it may or may not change."

At this point, pause and allow your partner to just be in contact with their inner experience. After about a minute, go back ask the first question, "What sensation are you aware of in your body right now?"
Cycle through the entire set of questions again.
If in this next cycle your partner offers answers like, "It is

in the same place" or "It's still the same," ask them to pretend you are asking them for the first time, and to give you a fresh description as if they are noticing it for the first time.

Keep cycling through the entire set of questions. In most cases, the sensations flow and change, and there comes a time when it seems right to finish the process.

Now we will look at the role of Flow Through:

THE ROLE OF FLOW THROUGH

- Move beyond the story
- Experience body sensations
- Patiently embrace whatever sensations come up, as you would hold a child
- Report qualities and changes in:
  shape - size - pressure - temperature
  weight - texture - movement - color

Most of us have difficulty with upset emotions. Some of us stuff or suppress such feelings. We may deny feeling anything at all. Others deal with upset by getting stuck in the story of what caused the upset. This story usually includes blame, criticism and other things that lead us to the Hole.

Consequently, upset feelings often end up getting stored in our bodies. We may carry them around for days, or even years. This can affect our health and well-being. It will also continue to affect our love and relationship.

It is important to overcome our resistance to embracing the so-called "negative"or "dark" emotions within us. They offer us immense value, and are well worth the discomfort we may initially have being with them. In connecting with these unwanted emotions, we connect with long banished parts of ourself.

Think about the lotus when you are afraid of the darkness inside of yourself—that which you normally avoid.

In Eastern culture, the lotus flower is thought to have the highest spiritual qualities—of clarity and enlightenment. When we see it, our hearts may be warmed with the feeling of, "Ah, such blissful peace!"

Consider the lotus flower a teacher on your journey to transformation and wholeness. Its roots sink deeply into a muddy, murky substance. It draws nourishment from this deep dark place, grows upward through water toward the sun, and blossoms in its radiant flower form—offering love and delight to all who gaze upon it.

Learn to embrace your inner world as the lotus plant embraces the mud below. This is the very material that is transformed into nourishment, healing, love and wholeness. Your embrace is what transforms it so.

The Flow Through process is a way of preventing and even unraveling our emotional gridlock. Instead of pushing away feelings or getting stuck in the story, we meet emotions in a fresh, new way that leads to transformation.

Think about the word "emotion" for a moment. E-Motion. "E" stands for Energy. "Energy in Motion."

Emotions are connected with the movement of energy through the body. We can block this flow of energy. In fact, we normally do so when we stuff our feelings or get stuck in our stories.

But we can also tap into the flow of emotions on the level of movement of energy. And this has the power to heal us and make us more whole. To start this energetic flow, we need to move beyond the story and into the body.

Let's start by summarizing the major skills involved in the process of Flow Through:

1. EXPERIENCE YOUR BODY SENSATIONS. In Flow Through, you are called on to focus on the exact sensations in your body right now. Get very specific and stay in the moment.

Sensations are the building blocks of emotions. They are the basic elements. Paying attention on this elemental level connects us with the flow of energy and transformation.

You start with whatever you are aware of in terms of body sensations. An example might be the feeling of tightness in one's stomach or throat. You might say, "I have a knot in my stomach" or a "lump in my throat."

2. EMBRACE WHATEVER COMES UP. Much of the time, we would prefer not to experience upset feelings—or the body sensations that correspond to them. This attitude can block our emotions from flowing, and hence they get stuck in our bodies—and psyches.

You will get a lot more from the role of Flow Through if you take a different attitude. Consider the following analogy when it comes to how to be with your feelings. Imagine that you have a six year old child. You love them very much and are an ideal parent. You are sitting inside the house reading, and they come in the front door. They are feeling upset in some way, due to something that happened to them outside. As that ideal parent, what would you do?

Choose among the following options for how you would greet this precious child. Would you:

- **Tell them to leave**
- **Send them to their room**
- **Tell them to go away 'til they feel okay**
- **Say they shouldn't feel that way**
- **Tell them to stop feeling that way**
- **Take on their feelings and start feeling the same way yourself**
- **Just embrace and hold them**

Most of us know in our hearts that ideally we would just embrace and hold that child with total love.

This is the way Flow Through asks you to greet the sensations that come up in your body. Don't "send them away" by not accepting them into your space. Just let them in and hold them in your awareness. Embrace the experience, as if it were a child you loved very much.

One key thing that can help is to breathe!

Embracing your inner feelings is an ultimate act of self-nurturing and self-love. It is a pathway to inner transformation and wholeness. It's an emotional skill that can transform and move a stuck relationship.

3. REPORT THE QUALITIES AND CHANGES. Flow Through is about staying connected with the movement of emotionally transformative energies. You do this by reporting to your partner about the qualities of your body sensations.

The questions that your partner, as Witness, will ask are designed to fine-tune your attention to your body sensations. You will be asked to describe their basic qualities, and how these qualities change over time.

Here are the qualities of sensation:

- **Location**
- **Size**
- **Shape**
- **Weight**
- **Temperature**
- **Density**
- **Pressure**
- **Motion**
- **Texture**
- **Color**

Take your time and just notice whatever you notice for each question. There is no "right" answer. You may not be able to answer all the questions, and that's okay.

If you even get a sense of something, just go with it. The point is to connect to whatever is going on inside of you. Embrace it. Let it be alive in any form it takes.

If you get more specific images, report those. Some people get colorful images of shapes that can even become recognizable. It is your experience. The important thing is to accept it and move with it.

When your partner asks you the same questions, even if nothing seems to have changed, report your experience as if it were fresh and new. Avoid just saying something like "It's still the same." Reset your focus and intention to truly embrace what is within you anew.

SUSPEND JUDGMENT

The Flow Through process allows us a different way of experiencing emotions: being present, breathing, and allowing them the time and space to flow through you. It is the process of moving beyond our normal stories or attempts to avoid feelings.

In moving beyond the mental level, to feel your feelings, you are called upon to continually suspend your judgment. For each thing that comes up, you are asked to simply accept it, as it is—and not want it to be different, or even to "mean" something. Simply allow experience to happen.

There is a Taoist story of an old farmer who had worked for many years. One day his horse ran away. Upon hearing the news, his neighbors came to visit. "Such bad luck," they said sympathetically. "We'll see," the farmer replied.

The next morning the horse returned, bringing with it three other wild horses. "How wonderful," the neighbors exclaimed. "We'll see," replied the old man.

The following day, his son tried to ride one of the untamed horses, was thrown, and broke his leg. The neighbors again came to offer their sympathy on his misfortune. "We'll see," answered the farmer.

The day after, military officials came to the village to draft young men into the army. Seeing that the son's leg was broken, they passed him by. The neighbors congratulated the farmer on how well things had turned out.

"We'll see," said the farmer.

In Flow Through, be like the farmer. Let sensations and emotions flow without trying to evaluate them. If something starts to come up, a part of you may want to label it, control it, or even keep it on hold if it appears to be "negative." But be like the old farmer and just say, "We'll see..."

A STREAM THAT FLOWS INTO TRANSFORMATION

Are there any feelings you hesitate to fully experience— like anger, hurt, sadness, fear, or grief? How do you try to avoid them? Have you ever noticed that when you don't let emotions flow through you, they tend to stick around?

A flowing stream can teach us much about how emotions naturally move. At times a stream runs shallow—at others, it runs deep. Sometimes it is gentle and slow, sometimes it reaches the intensity of white-water rapids. Yet a stream just keeps moving, even over rocks. Constantly flowing, it soon returns home to the ocean.

Flow Through encourages you to let your feelings flow. Feelings move like water. It's best to let them keep flowing— not to hold on, hold back, or try to stop midstream. If you open your heart and embrace feelings, all will be safe.

Confucius is said to have been visiting a great waterfall, which fell a height of two hundred feet. Its foam reached fifteen miles away and not even fish could survive entering it. Yet Confucius saw an old man go in, and concluded he was suffering from troubles and wanted to end his life.

Miraculously, the old man came out alive and unharmed downstream, and with flowing hair went carolling along the bank. Confucius followed him and said, "I had thought, sir, you were a spirit, but now I see you are a man. Kindly tell me, how did you survive this water?"

"I have been going into these waters since I was a small boy. Plunging in with the whirl, I come out with the swirl. I accommodated myself to the water, not the water to me. Without thinking, I allow myself to be shaped by it. And so I am able to deal with it after this fashion."

FLOW WITH THE STREAM

By not holding back, you won't keep feelings dammed up inside of you. If you don't push against them, they will remain free to move and flow like water, all the way through to transformation.

Do you recognize when you're pushing against a feeling? Can you tell when you are blocking an emotion or stuffing a feeling? Do you know when you're stuck in the story?

One indication is that you are trying to solve emotional problems through the mental realm. You become engaged in reasoning, judging, comparing, criticizing, blaming, labeling, justifying, ruminating, or rationalizing. But what you are not doing is simply feeling.

It's a bit like standing on the diving board, about to take the plunge. Experienced divers may engage in a brief mental preparation, like reviewing a short visualization of the dive they are about to perform. But beginners may get stuck in mental activity and never jump in.

We have all witnessed young people frozen on the edge of the board, unable to move any further. From our vantage point, we know they will be perfectly safe. Yet their fear of making the leap holds them back.

It requires a leap of faith to do Flow Through. We have been conditioned to fear many of our so-called negative emotions. We may literally believe we cannot survive if we allow ourselves to fully feel them.

So instead, we stand on the diving board, staying high and dry—in our heads, engaged in mental activities—as if that were actually going to resolve the emotional issue!

ENTER THE WATER

Flow Through invites you to fully feel your emotions. Rather than staying in your mind, move your awareness down into your heart, chest, neck, and belly—to simply experience whatever you feel.

Meet it. Accept it. Breathe deeply. Embrace it. And just feel it. Without words. Without the need for it to vanish or go away. Feel it as if it's the only thing you have left to do in this lifetime.

If feelings are a stream, then dive in and immerse yourself entirely—and be thoroughly cleansed! You will be safe. You can learn to flow with the stream and enjoy water.

Remember the advice that the old man gave to Confucius about negotiating the rushing river falls, "Plunge in with the whirl—accommodate yourself to the waters, not the waters to you."

Remember the old farmer, and suspend the temptation to mentally evaluate whether you should take the plunge or not. Delay judging what you are beginning to feel. Just say, "We'll see..."

Remember the analogy of the young child, for whom you are the ideal parent. The child arrives upset. All you have to do is embrace the child. Apply the attitude of an ideal and loving parent to the emotions that arrive within yourself, and embrace their presence.

As you fully embrace your feelings, you will begin to appreciate their presence as friends—as long lost parts of yourself. You will be like the lotus, sinking your roots deeply into that dark substance that nurtures your soul.

As your sensations move and flow, one feeling may lead to a different, still deeper feeling. This may then lead to yet another, perhaps lighter, feeling.

In this way, like a stream, the energy of emotion travels along its natural path to transformation.

FLOW THROUGH WITH A PARTNER

Letting feelings flow freely in the presence of a partner can support positive transformation—or it can lead to major turmoil! If your partner is willing and able to witness your feelings, it can be very healing indeed.

When they are so willing, and you are taking the role of Flow Through, beware of the tendency to stay in the mental arena. Beware of attaching any verbal labels, causes, reasons, or blame to what you feel.

Avoid going on and on about the story of what upsets you. Breathe in and out—and leave all the talk behind. The talk is only keeping you from the transformative experience of Flow Through, and potentially triggering your partner.

Simply experience your feelings, without a lot of words. If you can't do this, it would be better to stop, and come back to doing Flow Through again later.

When couples try to work out their problems by talking and talking, having the same discussion over and over again, there is probably an underlying emotional issue that is not ever being touched.

Flow Through is an entirely new road to travel. If you can do it with your partner, you will find a level of transformation and soulful connection that you never imagined possible.

FLOW THROUGH WITH A FRIEND

Not all couples are ready to do Flow Through with each other. But this should not stop you from using this powerful technique to transform your own negative feelings.

If your partner is not ready to partake in this process, it is equally beneficial to do Flow Through with a friend. Be there for one another in this very heartfelt way—and accompany each other in your transformation.

The process in partnering with a friend is identical to the technique we have just described.

If you want to transform your own negative feelings, you would call and ask your friend if they were willing to be a Witness for you. If they were available, you would then make an appointment to get together for the purpose of doing a Flow Through process.

It is best to set up a clear agreement with a friend about doing Flow Throughs. We advise a two-way agreement, where either of you can ask the other person to be a Witness for a Flow Through process.

EXERCISE — "YES" AND "NO" SIGNALS

Before you do an emotional Flow Through, we recommend you practice it on a simple test case. Get a little experience first working in this new way with feelings.

It may take a little practice to learn to be in touch with your body sensations—and to ask the cycle of questions we gave earlier.

So get together with your friend or partner for this test

case. Pick who is Flow Through and who is Witness. You will eventually trade roles, so just pick who goes first.

When you take the Flow Through role, your task is to describe the body sensations that occur when you have a total 100% "Yes!" response.

Imagine you are being given the chance to get a thing or an opportunity you truly want. It could be a great car, a wonderful vacation—anything at all. And price is no object, because imagine you have all the resources you ever need.

Imagine you are being asked if this is what you want.

And imagine you now get a clear, distinct "Yes!" response inside yourself. There is no ambiguity or doubt. It is a full-on total 100% "Yes!"

When you have the sense of that response, signal your Witness partner and it's time for them to begin asking the questions. Go through a few cycles of the questions.

When you have finished, switch roles and you be Witness for your friend to get in touch with their "Yes!" response.

If you are both interested, do another practice on what your internal "No!" response is. Pick a situation or context in which you absolutely do not want the option presented you— when you have a 100% total "No!" response.

FLOW THROUGH BY YOURSELF

Ultimately, the process of Flow Through is a gift that you give to yourself. It is not just for the sake of a relationship— nor is it merely a communication technique.

Flow Through is a practice that enables you to transform your negative internal states. It is a practice that helps you to heal inner wounds and to become more whole yourself. By embracing the full inner spectrum of emotions, you unblock yourself and your ability to fully experience love.

With this in mind, start doing Flow Through now—even if you aren't yet in a love relationship, or even if your current mate or a friend isn't ready to do it with you.

While having a partner to do this process with is great, you can still master it by yourself. Flow Through is ultimately a self-transformative process. A Witness can help focus you on your internal sensations and help hold a space for you—but when it comes down to it, you are doing the work.

WHEN TO DO A FLOW THROUGH. Do this process any time you are aware of negative thoughts or feelings.

Many of us are more focused in our thoughts, so negative feelings will often first show up in the mental realm. For instance: worry, fretting, nervous activity, rehashing a situation that didn't go as you wanted, criticizing, blaming or judging someone, including yourself, something churning away at you, being confused, inability to decide something.

These are only a few things that indicate that negative emotions are running your thoughts. And these are perfect opportunities to do a Flow Through.

HOW TO START. Find a time and place where you can just sit down, be alone and be quiet for at least 15 minutes.

Start by getting yourself as comfortable as possible. Notice your breathing, without changing it. Notice where you might have any tensions in your body. And notice what thoughts are running through your head.

Check in with how you are breathing regularly for the first couple of minutes, even as you may get caught up in what you are thinking. Do not try to change anything, just notice your breathing. Is it deep or shallow? Slow or fast? Is it in your chest or does it go down to your belly?

When you are ready, gradually shift your awareness into your body—into your chest and belly. Do the In & Down process (Chapter 8).

If thoughts capture your attention again, just gently return your attention to below your neck each time and notice if there are any sensations in your chest or belly, or in between.

Pay attention to whatever you feel below your neck.

Gradually get a sense of the precise location. Is it in your belly, or in your chest, or where is it exactly? Is it in the center line of your body or more to one side or the other?

Gradually get a sense of the various qualities it has. What is it's shape? Is it heavy or light? Is it moving or still? Is it warm or cool? Start with those questions and refine your sense of the sensations you are sitting with.

BE YOUR IDEAL INNER PARENT. Now get a sense of the relationship you have with these sensations. This is the essence of your relationship with yourself.

And you can change it—right now.

What is your attitude towards these inner sensations? Is it welcoming or wishing they would go away? Are you willing to embrace these sensations or are you gritting your teeth?

Pretend for the moment these sensations are those of a child you love very much, who is coming into your room.

Can you remember what the ideal parent would do? If you

were the ideal parent, would you send this child to their room? Would you mimic their upset feelings? Or would you make space for them, simply embrace them and allow them to feel whatever they feel?

For a moment, relax into just allowing these sensations to be in that room with you—the inner room of your body—and make room for them to be whatever they are.

Will you survive if you just allow these sensations to exist within you for a moment more, without wishing them away?

Find out.

Allow them space to simply be. Find out what happens. Embrace them as if they were a little child. Become the space that surrounds these sensations.

Move your awareness to a spot a few inches to the right of these sensations. What does it feel like there? Notice how it is different than being inside the sensations.

Then move your awareness to a few inches to the left of the sensations. What does it feel like there?

Then expand your awareness so that you are the space that is to both sides, above and below, in front of and behind, totally surrounding these sensations.

Be that space that surrounds these sensations.

Can you hold the space for the sensations to just be?

Allow, breathe into that space, and just notice whatever happens next.

BE PATIENT. You might not be able to do a tenth of the things suggested above the first time you do Flow Through. So be very patient with yourself and know that whatever you are doing is absolutely the right thing.

Read the suggestions above as a map of possible places to visit, and take your time wherever you happen to be. There is not ultimate single correct destination.

As you do more and more Flow Throughs, you become more adept at refined inner sensing. This is like any skill based behavior. You get better and more flexible at doing it the more you do it.

So start now—and know there are only two things you really need to succeed in doing Flow Through.

Curiosity will be your strongest ally.

That and acceptance.

Everyone does Flow Through different. So why shouldn't you do it your own unique way, too?

The two keys to success are curiosity and acceptance.

Curiosity to actively explore what is within you.

And acceptance of what you find.

NO JUDGMENTS—NO GOALS. Remember again the farmer. Instead of having certain expectations or goals, take a "We'll see..." attitude. Be open to whatever happens.

In Flow Through, often the result is a subtle shift within yourself as you continue to embrace the sensations inside your body. This shift is a transformation, an opening to a new possibility, a slight healing of something old.

Sometimes you may simply notice a sigh or that your breathing has shifted in some subtle way.

At other times, the shifts you will experience will be clear and quite large in magnitude. You may feel energy moving through your body in an almost electrical way. You may see striking images that correspond to this energy. You may later notice you feel and act differently in a situation that normally triggers you into negativity.

Sometimes the shifts are quite subtle.

Sometimes they are strong and carry us to new levels of inner healing, peace or strength.

Allow whatever you get to be right—because it is.

Do not expect that all Flow Throughs will feel or end up the same way.

They won't.

Each is unique.

In fact, let go of goals and expectations.

Just wait and see.

Bring with you curiosity and acceptance.

RESULTS OF FLOW THROUGH

The act of doing Flow Throughs is an act of self-love.

No matter what specific results you get in any particular session, the net effect is that you are demonstrating to yourself on deeper and deeper levels your own self-love.

This self-love is what transforms you.

On a most basic level, doing Flow Through is a way to learn to better tolerate and be with negative emotions.

Why is this desirable?

When we are not able to tolerate feelings like anger or pain within ourselves, we will do one of two things. We will either try to suppress these feelings and avoid them. Or we will try to eject the feelings and act them out with our partner. Both of these strategies damage love and hurt us.

These two strategies—suppression or ejection—are what

takes us into the Hole. They are based on the "fight or flight" response. Only instead of this fear-based reaction being to a tiger in the jungle—it is the fear of an emotion coming up within us.

The ability to embrace and become the space in which all our feelings can come up is what transforms us. We gain a tolerance to inner emotions and an ability to soothe our own feelings.

This takes the pressure off our relationship to do the inner work that, in reality, only we can do.

It is a myth and self-defeating stance of today that our love relationship should "make" us feel happy and "take care" of us when we do not. Adhering to this stance spells the doom of a healthy relationship and a commitment to codependency.

By doing Flow Through—with a partner or by ourselves— we reverse this trend. We show up and take responsibility for our own feelings. And in doing so, we arrive at a new quality of relationship with ourself.

The shift in our inner relationship to self-care and self-love is the core transformation that makes us more whole. Doing a Flow Through is a direct demonstration to yourself of your own commitment to self-love and self-nurturing.

As you do each practice of Flow Through, you will touch certain parts of yourself that have longed for you attention. It could be a part that was hurt long ago in childhood, that brings up with it certain sensitivities today.

In the act of paying attention to this part of yourself with an attitude of self-caring—you are healing yourself.

Over time you will notice that you spend far less time needing to process negative feelings in relationships. You will feel more whole and happy within yourself. The way in which you communicate with others will become more effective and constructive.

And the choices you make in love will be more wise.

CHAPTER ELEVEN

CREATE A POWERFUL SHARED VISION

"You've got to be very careful if you don't know where you are going because you might not get there."
—YOGI BERRA

We will now bring together the various tools of this book. You will see how they can be coordinated in the context of a plan to go forward.

In essence, we will be describing a Shared Vision contract that a couple can make. Such a contract is based on the highest intentions each partner has.

It is a mutual contract to have a conscious relationship— and it will support each person to bring out their best when they are in the midst of relationship challenges.

A Shared Vision contract makes a clear statement of how you plan to work with problems and upsets in a way that is congruent with your higher intentions.

It is a plan for success in navigating the sometimes difficult terrain of human love and intimacy.

We will look at how one couple, David and Lisa, created such a contract to support their shared vision of "Growth." As we discuss their process, consider which agreements you would include in your own contract.

The first part of their contract was to acknowledge that they each carried baggage from the past into the relationship. This was a commitment to their mutual willingness to claim and own their past baggage.

1. BOTH PARTNERS ADMIT THEY HAVE:

- Sensitivities
- Limited clarity
- Room to improve communication
- Differences, and that's okay
- Emotional wounds from the past
- Unrealized parts of self

David and Lisa started by admitting they each did, in fact, have sensitivities, limits, wounds, fears and old patterns. Each admitted that there were areas where they could grow and become more whole. They acknowledged they were different in some ways, and each said that was okay.

This agreement made it safer for them to claim baggage with each other, which was a vital part of their growth. They realized they were in partnership around personal growth and that each, in their own way, had to grow.

This led them to the next part of their contract, where they made an agreement that neither one of them was "right" or the other "wrong."

2. AGREE NO ONE IS "RIGHT"

- Move beyond blame & name-calling
- There's no identified "problem" person
- It's a "no-fault" partnership

Essentially, both David and Lisa agreed to move beyond judging or blaming each other, as a matter of first principle.

This didn't mean that they never reverted to pointing the finger again. It was, however, a formal statement that each of them recognized that judging and blaming were destructive. Saying this helped them see when they were doing it—and to stop doing it.

They also agreed that there would not be an identified problem person in the relationship. They embraced the fact that relating is like dancing, and that both partners were fully participating in whatever was happening.

In this sense, they adopted a "no-fault" partnership. Why wait for a no-fault divorce, when you can have a no-fault relationship? When you take away blame, you can more easily find the path to growth and happiness.

Next, David and Lisa explored mutual growth goals—of healing old wounds, expanding beyond their current limits, and finding greater personal wholeness.

3. JOIN IN THE MUTUAL GOALS OF:
- Healing old wounds
- Growing beyond old limits
- Finding greater wholeness

The way both David and Lisa spelled out "Growth" came to include some of the other words used for higher intentions. "Healing" applied to old wounds. "Wholeness" applied to areas that frequently gave rise to conflict.

It turned out that many of their conflicts arose from differences between them in the emotional arena. David was quite comfortable feeling and expressing anger. He was from a family where members would raise their voices in anger, yet still knew they loved and cared for each other.

Lisa had a different background, and she had vowed at an early age to avoid anger at all costs because it caused so much pain. She typically would grow silent and distant around a show of anger, or anything that might cause it, and would also tend to suppress her own anger.

In the relationship, anger had become a trigger of upset, judgment and blame. David was triggered by Lisa's distancing when he was upset. He also was concerned with her failure to express anger. At the same time, Lisa judged David to be "wrong" for showing anger, and felt a lot of old pain when he expressed it.

Interestingly enough, when it came to another emotion, that of sadness, the situation was reversed. Although Lisa couldn't tolerate or feel anger, she was easily able to feel and express sadness. David, on the other hand, was trained to believe it less than manly to express sadness. He had learned to deny this human emotion within himself.

4. FOR EMOTIONAL GROWTH:

- All feelings are okay to feel (anger - hurt - sadness - fear)
- But NOT all ways of expressing these feelings are okay
- Make agreements about ways to express feelings

Eventually, they saw this pattern of emotional gridlock.

Their higher intentions included "Wholeness" and they spelled out supporting agreements in the emotional arena.

They agreed that all feelings were okay. That meant that anger and sadness are both okay. They agreed that a whole person would be able to feel and express both emotions.

If anger is "red" and sadness is "blue" then they were, in effect, saying that a part of their personal growth is getting access to the complete spectrum, to have all the colors included in their emotional rainbows.

David and Lisa both admitted being cut off from a vital part of their own spectrum. Each acknowledged that many of their conflicts simply reflected their own personal lack of emotional wholeness. Thus both of them embraced the value of allowing all feelings to be okay.

In saying all feelings are okay to feel, they were not saying that all ways of expressing those feelings were okay. Lisa agreed that feeling angry was okay—but behaviors like touching each other in angry ways like pushing, grabbing or hitting certainly was not. And throwing things was not okay. David said that feeling sad was okay, but waking the other person up at two in the morning to try to resolve it was not.

They spent some time discussing other situations where anger or sadness might come up—and what behaviors would be okay or not okay in each case. Lisa suggested alternative ways David could express his anger that would work better for her. He told her ways to ask for his support when she was feeling sad. They also stated their support of one another in growing emotionally more whole.

The last part of their agreement explored ways to work with upsets and challenges as they came up.

5. AGREE TO TAKE A NEW ROAD WITH UPSETS AND CHALLENGES:

- Use upsets as material for growth
- Have a Time Out agreement
- Master In & Down to get centered
- Use the Talker-Listener tool
- Do Baggage Claim for healing
- Use Flow Through to heal and transform negative emotions
- Get support from a third party

This is the real heart of the contract. It brings together all the tools and commits to using them.

Here, David and Lisa agree to use anything upsetting or challenging as material for growth. They pledge to explore new strategies and do whatever it takes to work through challenges.

To back this up, they made specific agreements for what they will do.

They will use a Time Out agreement (Chapter 7). They will use the Flow Through process (Chapter 10) for healing old wounds and transforming upset emotions. They committed to do Talker-Listener sessions (Chapter 9), as a way to come back after a "Time Out"—or as a method to keep the communication lines open. They will use In & Down (Chapter 8) to stay resourceful, or to calm themselves if they lose it. Finally, they agreed to use third party help whenever they got stuck and could not work things out themselves.

When they first arrived, David and Lisa were on the verge of splitting up. Their patterns, especially the emotional gridlock, created a great deal of pain and suffering. As a couple, they spent a lot of time in the Hole. They had no idea that there was any other road they could take.

Committing to the Shared Vision contract around their higher intentions of "Growth" was a dramatic turning point in David and Lisa's love life.

TIME PERIOD FOR THE CONTRACT

David and Lisa committed to staying with their contract, no matter what came up—for a period of one year.

It makes sense that a couple commit to a minimum of six months, to really give themselves the chance to master the tools and integrate them into the relationship.

All too often, a couple keeps a highly negative question in their focus—like whether to stay together or split up. Staying intent on that kind of question keeps each partner from doing their personal growth work—work which could completely transform the quality of the relationship.

You will get more if you put all of your focus on your highest positive intention for yourself personally. In the midst of the challenges and upsets, by keeping focus on personal growth, wholeness or healing, you will mature and become more resourceful as a human.

Consider the alternative: stewing in the negative question, blaming your partner for the mess, and needing them to change so you can feel better. This will get the relationship nowhere. And you will not grow one bit.

When you shift your focus to your higher intention, and commit to a contract aligned with this, mountains can move.

Over the years, I have witnessed couples co-create results that often seem miraculous.

RESULTS OF SHARED VISION CONTRACT

- Partners embrace upset feelings
- Emotional learning happens
- Ownership of feelings
- Less blaming the other person
- Less acting out of emotions
- Less destructive communication
- Reduced influence of past baggage
- Past wounds & resentments healed
- Relationship is kept clear
- Feelings operate as balanced and appropriate signals in the present

As couples travel down a new road such as "Growth," challenges are more easily faced. Upset is no longer a signal that it's time to retreat or attack, no longer a reason to think the relationship is bad or the other person is wrong. Instead, partners start to embrace challenges as opportunities for personal growth.

This enables emotional learning to happen. Partners learn to own their feelings, instead of blaming the other person or acting out. Our baggage and the 95% factor decreases in power as past wounds are healed. Old patterns are dropped.

The relationship is cleared of built up resentments and emotional gridlock—and it stays clear. Feelings are appropriate to events in the present rather than being contaminated or amplified by the past.

Operating on the 5% level, partners can express and respond to each other constructively. Communicating on the 5% level works. You can successfully negotiate wants and needs, and find mutually satisfying solutions to challenges.

Once you have committed yourself to a Shared Vision, you have a clear motivation to operate on the 5% level and not fall into the 95%. You are motivated to use communication techniques that support your journey down a new road.

RELATIONSHIP AND GROWTH

Relationships are our greatest teacher. They tell us what we need to learn next in life to grow as individuals. We are called upon to expand our souls, heal our past wounds and evolve as humans.

Love is that which brings up our lesson plan.

A lasting and satisfying relationship will naturally involve you in your own inner personal growth. Moving through upsetting challenges is a normal part of this growth.

When you commit to a Shared Vision, you become partners on a conscious journey of your own making, a co-explorer of a new path.

Committing to a Shared Vision will inspire you to show up in a new way when both of you get stuck in upset or negativity. It will be a conscious reminder to embrace the upsets, to learn how to expand yourself and elevate the troubling situation.

In the work of relationship, when the honeymoon's over you are called on to instigate positive transformation. You are asked to co-create and take a new path with your partner.

Each partner needs to come forward in times of challenge and expand, rather than close down. The main thing preventing us from doing this work is that we haven't had a healthy role model for how to do it.

We are sadly lacking in useful guidelines for doing the work of relationship. We have few understandings that lift us to transform, much less resolve, our upsets.

Most of us were raised in families which did not model how to positively resolve the challenges in relationship. We have seldom seen it done well, and may not even know a couple that can do it.

On the contrary, we mostly see and talk about couples who are stuck in drama or unhappiness. We know couples who are doing a lot of work—that does not work!

Because of the abysmal state of love and relationship that runs throughout our society, it is becoming clear that we need to learn to do a new kind of relationship work. Let's start this now, and forge our own definition of "right partner."

How do you know when you are truly with the right partner?

It's not a matter of magic feelings. It's very simple:

You know you're with the right partner when you are both consciously doing your personal growth in the relationship.

This means that you can only find out if you're with a true partner by going through times of challenge or upset. You cannot gauge it by the honeymoon phase alone.

To know if you are with a true partner, you need to see how you both show up and consciously "work" with upsets, sensitivities, differences and challenges.

Unfortunately, many potentially great couples get lost because they don't know how to do relationship work. They don't know the tools in this book. Instead, they hold onto the popular unconscious myth of "true love"—where upset feelings shouldn't happen, where upset is a bad sign.

Or couples may work real hard, by talking a problem in circles. They exhaust their hearts in ineffective unconscious strategies—until they finally give up or split up.

Many people feel they have already met a life partner, but then, somehow, lost them. One man at a talk we were giving sadly said, "I was with someone who felt like my soulmate ten years ago. I just don't know what happened. I can't get her out of my mind."

At the end of the talk, after we had discussed the power of having a personal and shared vision, he said, "I realize now that I just did not have an effective, conscious way to work with our problems. I thought that there was nowhere to go but down. I wish I'd heard this talk a decade ago."

Something clicked for him. He realized that the future held the possibility of another love, and that it was crucial for him to consciously commit to his personal growth now, even as he was still single.

Now is always the best time to commit to a personal intention for how to see challenges and upsets. Regardless of whether you are in a significant relationship or not, you have an opportunity to put your highest intention into practice.

GREAT RELATIONSHIPS ARE GROWN... NOT FOUND

Ultimately, the quality of relationship you can have is directly linked to your willingness to engage in personal growth. It is linked to how willing you are to expand your mind and heart. And it is linked to how proactive you are in creating the love you want.

We live in a time that needs new models for relationship. The divorce rate remains high, decade after decade. Half of marriages end in pain. Certainly few of them began that way. A large percentage of divorced couples report deep regrets that they didn't know how to work things out.

Any work they tried to do—absolutely did *not* work!

Research is showing us interesting facts. Couples who stay together have as many issues as couples who split up. The difference is not the absence of conflict, but the strategies they bring to the table to work with the challenges that come up.

New strategies can be learned. Quality relating is not some abstract or unobtainable thing. Nor is it a matter of luck.

We need to revise our models of love and relating in a way that helps us face the challenges and see these as pathways to strengthen our love.

Challenges help us grow, as individuals and as couples.

There's a story about a group of kids who go for a walk and discover a cocoon. Fascinated, they gather and watch as the butterfly inside works hard to get free. A girl in the group

suggests they time the event. As the butterfly stretches and struggles, it pushes out of the cocoon, little by little.

The children groan with each push. Eventually, after an agonizing fifteen minutes, the butterfly breaks free and spreads its colorful wings in flight.

As the children continue to walk, they soon find a second cocoon. It also is in a state of excited movement. Having witnessed the first, one child sympathetically asks how they might help this second butterfly get free, faster.

"Why should it work so much?"

They agree. A boy takes out his pocketknife and gently makes a slit in the cocoon. Sure enough, the butterfly is able to flop out with little struggle, in less than two minutes!

But quickly it begins to contract and close up on itself. Within minutes it is dead.

Shocked, they later talk to their teacher, who explains it. The butterfly, in stretching and pushing against the cocoon, moves vital fluids into veinlike structures in its wings that strengthen its frame. The struggle is what allows the butterfly to complete its transformation from caterpillar into a magnificent flying creature. Only by fully engaging in the challenges of the cocoon can the butterfly ever spread its wings in flight.

So too, must we fully engage in the challenges that arise in love to actualize our true partnership potential.

DO IT NOW

As they say, "If not now—then when?"

If you have not yet decided on your higher intentions, we strongly recommend that you now commit to:

Personal Growth, Wholeness & Healing

Take some time now and expand your higher intentions into a set of specific new agreements, as was demonstrated by David and Lisa.

If you are in a relationship, and your partner is willing to join you, do this together within the next week.

If your partner is not willing—they may need time—then do this for yourself as a personal intention. It takes at least one partner to change the dynamics of a relationship. Do this now whether or not your partner is ready to join you.

If you are single, do this as your personal intention. You can also do this with a friend, family member or any meaningful relationship.

Committing to your highest intentions will change your life—and empower you to determine the direction that this change will take.

PERSONAL RESOLUTIONS

To prepare yourself to make a Shared Vision contract with a partner, read the following set of personal resolutions.

Edit this if you need to—then sign and date it.

I resolve the following, regarding relationship problems, differences between me and the other person, and upset or negative feelings that may come up:

It's okay to include problems, differences and upsets in a relationship as I learn to work with them, since they now exist whether I like it or not.

I am willing to see these as opportunities for myself to heal and grow personally.

I will learn to provide a safe space for healing and growth for both of us as partners.

I admit I may be unconscious of all that is involved when problems and upsets come up. For instance:

I may not remember in the moment the personal history of mine that is being triggered;

I may not be able to recognize that I am making false interpretations of you;

I may not know what emotional baggage I am carrying that is involved in my reaction to you.

I am willing to create a safe space to explore these things with you. I will discuss how we can create more safety to do our healing and growth together.

I intend to be a full and active partner in healing these things and growing personally.

This is so, regardless of the source of problems and upsets (you, me, the past, the present).

I will learn to better own and know within myself all my feelings.

I will learn to constructively express all my feelings.

I am willing to set up mutual guidelines as to what is constructive.

I will learn to better own and know within myself what I want or need.

I will learn to constructively express my wants.

I will learn to ask you to give me feedback.

I am willing to set up mutual guidelines as to what is constructive.

I am willing to explore and become aware of:

How I may be projecting my past onto you;

How I may be unconsciously polarizing with you over our differences;

How my negative judgments and labels are limiting our relationship potential.

I will become conscious of my defensive reactions, coping strategies and inner obstacles to intimacy.

I will summon the courage to do something different instead of my usual reactive patterns, so we can heal and grow together.

I will own the feelings I have and the wounds from my past that may be involved in my upsets.

I will continue to develop my full potential for wholeness as an individual.

I will empower you to develop your full potential for wholeness as an individual.

I will do this even if I feel anxious or insecure.

I will learn to own and take care of my troubling feelings instead of trying to get you to do that.

I will put more inner focus on how I can heal or grow and less outer focus on how you should change.

I will make happiness, acceptance and compassion a high priority for us to share.

Signed,

_____

Date: _____

Once you make personal resolutions like those above, you are ready to write a Shared Vision contract with a partner.

The following contract is based on what we presented earlier in this chapter. Feel free to edit or modify it as you discuss this with your partner.

It is important to commit to a certain period of time, like six to twelve months.

During this time, make the intentions of the Shared Vision your first priority. Keep a focus on your higher intentions, like "Growth" or "Healing."

If you are suffering from questions like "should we stay together?" put those on the back burner until after the contract period is up. Focusing on such questions will distract you from doing the personal growth and transformation work you have committed to do in the contract.

SHARED VISION CONTRACT

1. Both of us admit we have:
   - Sensitivities
   - Limited clarity
   - Room to improve communication
   - Differences, and that's okay
   - Emotional wounds from the past
   - Emotional hot buttons and triggers
   - Unrealized parts of ourselves

2. We agree that no one is "right"
   - We will move beyond blame or name-calling
   - There's no identified "problem" person
   - It's a "no-fault" partnership

3. We join in the mutual intentions of:
   - Healing old sensitivities, triggers and wounds
   - Expanding beyond old patterns and limits
   - Finding greater wholeness
   - _____

   (Write in any other higher intentions you have)

4. For emotional growth we agree:
   - All feelings are okay to feel (anger, hurt, fear)
   - But NOT all ways of expressing feelings are okay
   - We make new agreements for expressing feelings:

   _____

   (Write in agreements on expressing feelings)

5. We will take a "new road" when facing challenges:
   - We will use upsets as material for growth
   - We will use our Time Out agreement
   - We will use tools to get centered, like In & Down
   - We will use the Talker-Listener tool
   - We will do baggage claim for healing
   - We will use Flow Through to transform upsets
   - We will get support from a third party if needed

Time Period of Contract: _____

Starting Date: _____

Signed,

_____

_____

EPILOGUE
TAKE YOUR
NEXT STEP FORWARD

"A journey of a thousand miles begins with a single step."
— LAO TZU

Having read this far, you now have a powerful set of tools for creating and sustaining a rewarding partnership. But a tool can only be effective if you actually use it.

Depending on the state of your relationship, you may want to consider the option of getting third party coaching. This can help you stick to your Shared Vision contract and implement the tools over time into your relationship.

If you are open to outside help, know that it can take some shopping around to find the right person. There are many who offer relationship counseling, yet only a rare few who seem to know how to make a difference.

So find someone who actually helps you get results, and who understands the material in this book. You want coaching to help you master these tools, and apply them to resolve the problems that come up in your daily life.

People tend to wait for too long before getting help.

That can be a serious mistake.

Don't let pride or other false issues stand in your way.

However, if you do not feel you need outside help, that is okay. It puts the full responsibility on you to practice and integrate the tools in this book into your life.

That responsibility already rests in you, with or without third party help—so if you want to do it yourself, be sure to do it as seriously as you would build a house, for instance.

Learning and using new tools takes time.

Progress is not a straight line. Do not set yourself up for failure by expecting everything to improve quickly and without setbacks.

People learn things, make mistakes, forget to use the tools, blow it, pick themselves up again, move forward. That is real life. Be realistic. Just try to keep going two steps forward for every one you fall back.

You are gradually building new habits. It can be like going to the gym to work out. At first, you have to drag yourself there, and it is hard to even remember to make time. But after you have built a positive habit of working out, it feels easier to go to the gym than to sit around.

It will be like that exercising these tools, as they become solid habits. Eventually, you will not want to act out old reaction patterns. You will prefer to "work out"—so to speak— issues in your relationship using these healthier methods.

FINAL WORDS OF ADVICE

The basic rule to create change is simple—do something different (Chapter 6). Here are additional things to remember to do, as you integrate the tools in this book into your life:

GO IN & DOWN. Master the In & Down tool (Chapter 8) for soothing upset feelings. This is vital. The more you work with your own emotions, the less they will get dumped into your relationship. In & Down helps you stay centered and resourceful when things become potentially charged.

USE YOUR TIME OUT AGREEMENT. When upset, take a Time Out (Chapter 7). Do not short change yourself by going to the Hole. Do mock Time Outs for awhile, so you can get used to giving the signal. When you do get upset, do call a Time Out. Next, go In & Down to calm yourself. Then recall your highest intentions, and figure out what you want to communicate in a followup Talker-Listener session.

SET YOUR INTENTION. As much as possible, stay awake to your higher intentions (Chapter 2). When challenges come up, set your intention for yourself. For instance, if "Growth" is your highest personal intention, then see how you can grow in every challenging situation.

KNOW YOUR PERSONAL GROWTH. Stay aware of the growth for your personality type (Chapter 4). Act on it. Say and do things that represent this growth for you. Do not allow yourself to slip into old comfortable patterns. Go against your own grain, and expand beyond your own limits.

WATCH OUT FOR POLARITIES. Watch out for polarity dances in your relationship (Chapter 5). When you see one occur, figure out how you can do the opposite of what you normally do in order to restore balance to the relationship.

CLAIM YOUR BAGGAGE. Freely admit and claim how your past affects you (Chapter 3). Help your partner understand you better this way—and understand them better. Opening old baggage to the light of love can start a healing process. It also helps you be more sensitive to each other.

USE TALKER-LISTENER. Initiate discussions about issues with the Talker-Listener tool (Chapter 9). Learn to really listen. Learn to speak from the heart, clearly and with no judgements or blame. Always use this tool as a way to discuss charged issues, especially if you called a Time Out.

USE FLOW THROUGH. Learn to embrace and transform your own upset feelings (Chapter 10). Heal emotional wounds from the past that still affect you. Get skillful in using this tool, so you can take better care of your emotional arena. Doing this keeps your relationship clear of baggage.

STICK TO YOUR SHARED VISION. Do what you have committed to in the Shared Vision contract (Chapter 11). This contract is your job description. Stay close to the letter of the law you have laid down. Don't let yourself get sidetracked from the higher intentions you chose this contract to serve.

BE ALERT. What will get in the way of progress is your normal coping strategies and need for comfort. Each time you revert to your usual strategies, you will go to the Hole, and fail to move forward on the new road you truly intend.

When you fall back, reset your intention and use the tools in this book. Push against your old habitual patterns. Get out of the Hole as quickly as you can.

Then make a new move forward. All relationships have issues and challenges. Do not let these pull you into despair. Stay true to your Shared Vision contract—to your true highest intentions—and keep practicing the tools.

I wish you well on your journey!

NOTES

1. Alan Watts: *The Book*

2. Gregory Bateson: *Steps to an Ecology of Mind*

3. Helen Palmer: *The Enneagram in Love and Work*
   HarperSanFrancisco, 1996

4. David Daniels: *The Essential Enneagram*
   HarperSanFrancisco, 2000

The material in Chapter Four compiles information from the books and professional training programs of Helen Palmer and David Daniels. The In & Down exercise in Chapter Eight includes materials presented by Helen Palmer.

See their official Enneagram website for more information: www.authenticenneagram.com

ABOUT THE AUTHOR

John Grey received a Ph.D. in psychology in 1975 from Stanford, where he taught and codirected a National Science Foundation sponsored research center. Since 1980 he has been in private practice and teaching workshops focused on communication, relationship and personal growth.

For over 20 years John has provided effective, practical coaching to help people have healthy, joyful, rewarding relationships.

RELATIONSHIP COACHING BY PHONE AND COUPLES RETREATS

John offers relationship coaching to people throughout the United States by phone. He has an in-person private practice in Sonoma County, California.

He also conducts couples retreats in California. He has developed a unique intensive weekend program where couples are coached to resolve issues and transform their relationships using the tools in this book.

Information about these services—as well as free online self-help tools—can be found at the following website:

http://www. soulmateoracle. com

Printed in the United States
210593BV00001B/60/A